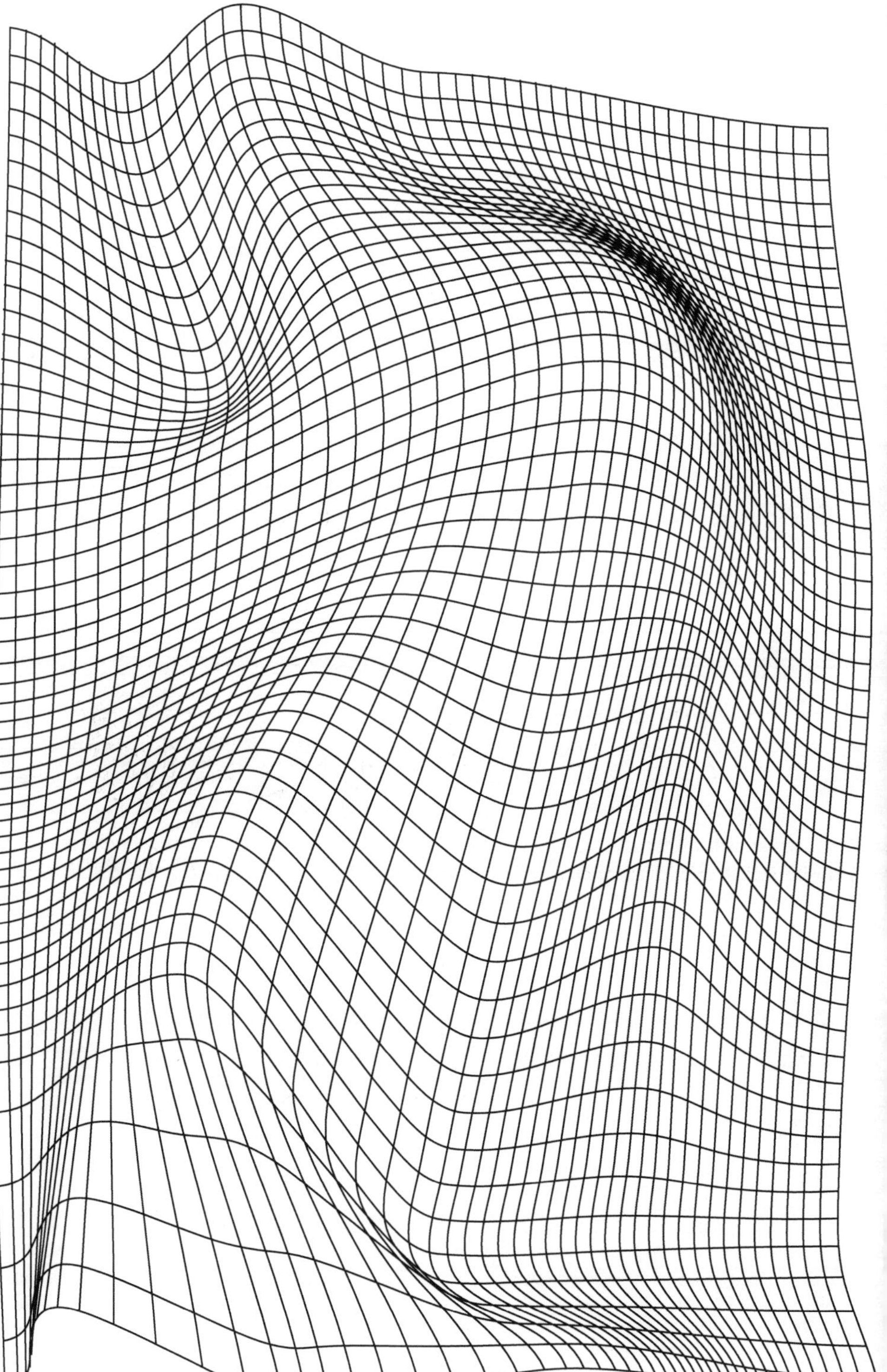

RECLAIM

Reclaim

Copyright © 2021 Lark. All rights reserved. Except for brief quotations in critical publications or reviews, no part of this book may be reproduced in any manner without prior written permission from the publisher.

ISBN: 9798741567173

Authors: Russ Johnson & Tony Sorci

Published by: Lark
larksite.com

LARK

Typesetting & Interior Design by: Tony Sorci
Cover Design by: Tony Sorci

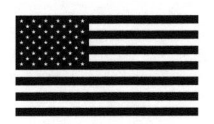

Manufactured in the U.S.A

Unless otherwise indicated, all Scripture quotations are from The Holy Bible, English Standard Version® (ESV®), copyright © 2001 by Crossway, a publishing ministry of Good News Publishers. Used by permission. All rights reserved.

This book is dedicated to the burdened and burned out.

May you find the freedom to be nothing in and of yourself as you pass on the Good News of God's reckless grace.

The Great Christian Revolutions Came Not By The Discovery Of Something That Was Not Known Before. They Happen When Someone Takes Radically Something That Was Always There.

Richard Niebuhr

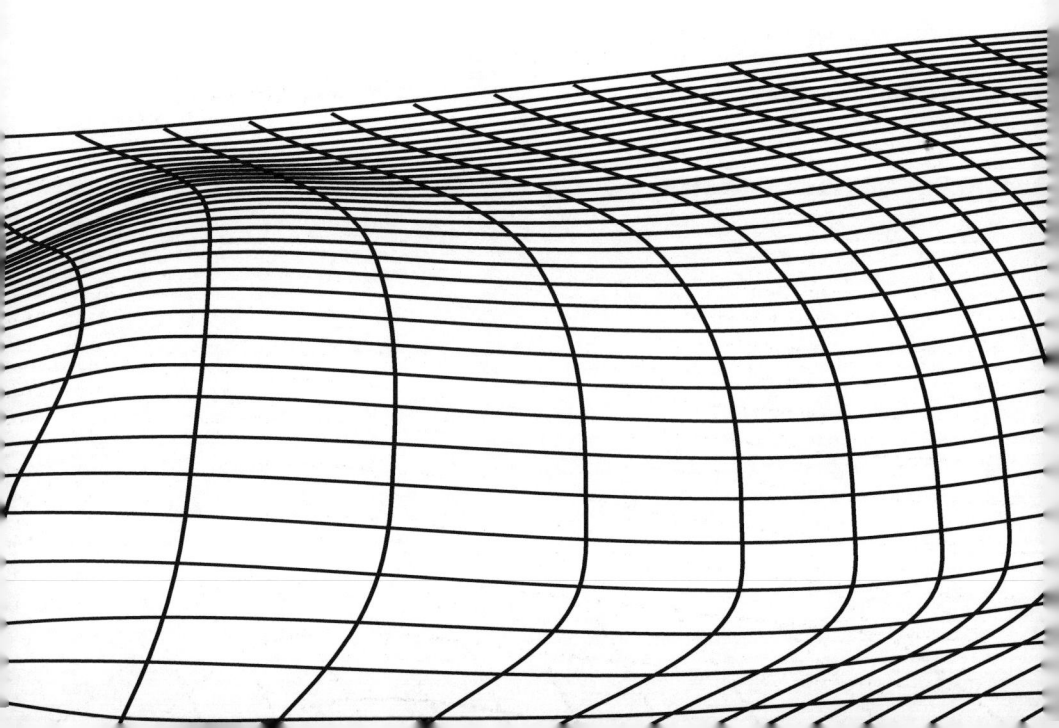

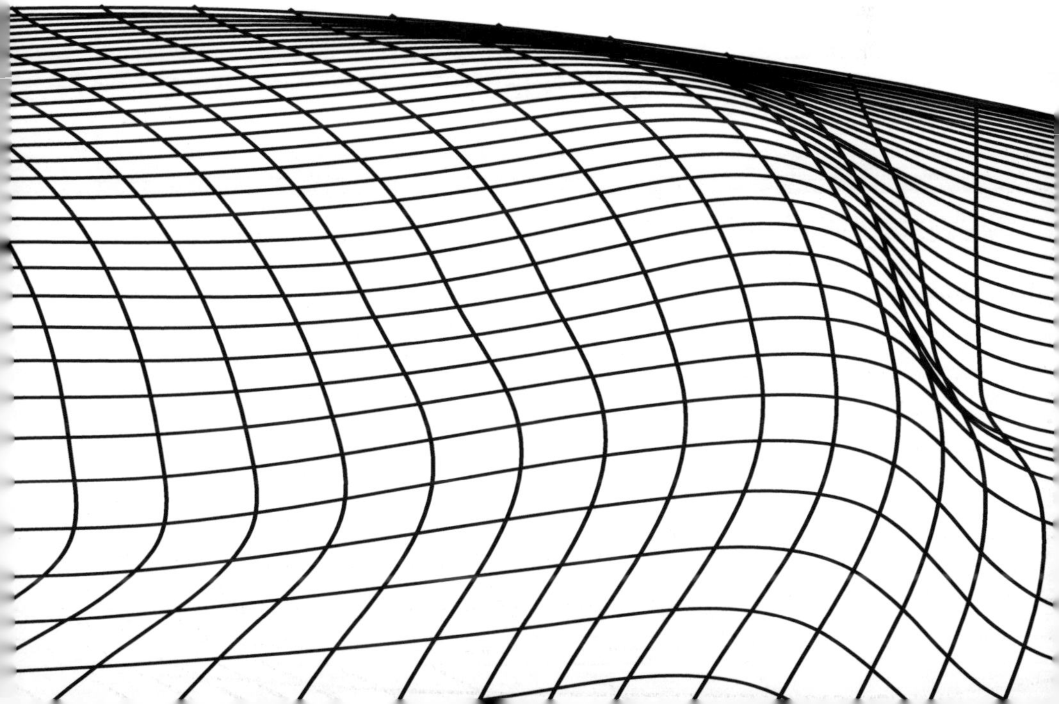

CONTENTS

About		12

Reclaim

0	Intro	17
1	Jesus	25
2	Cross	35
3	Trust	47
4	Rest	61
5	Walk	77
6	Church	91
7	Disciple	103
8	Spaces	117
9	Play	133

Reflect

1		148
2		150
3		152
4		154

5	156
6	158
7	160
8	162
9	164

About the Authors	168
About Lark	169

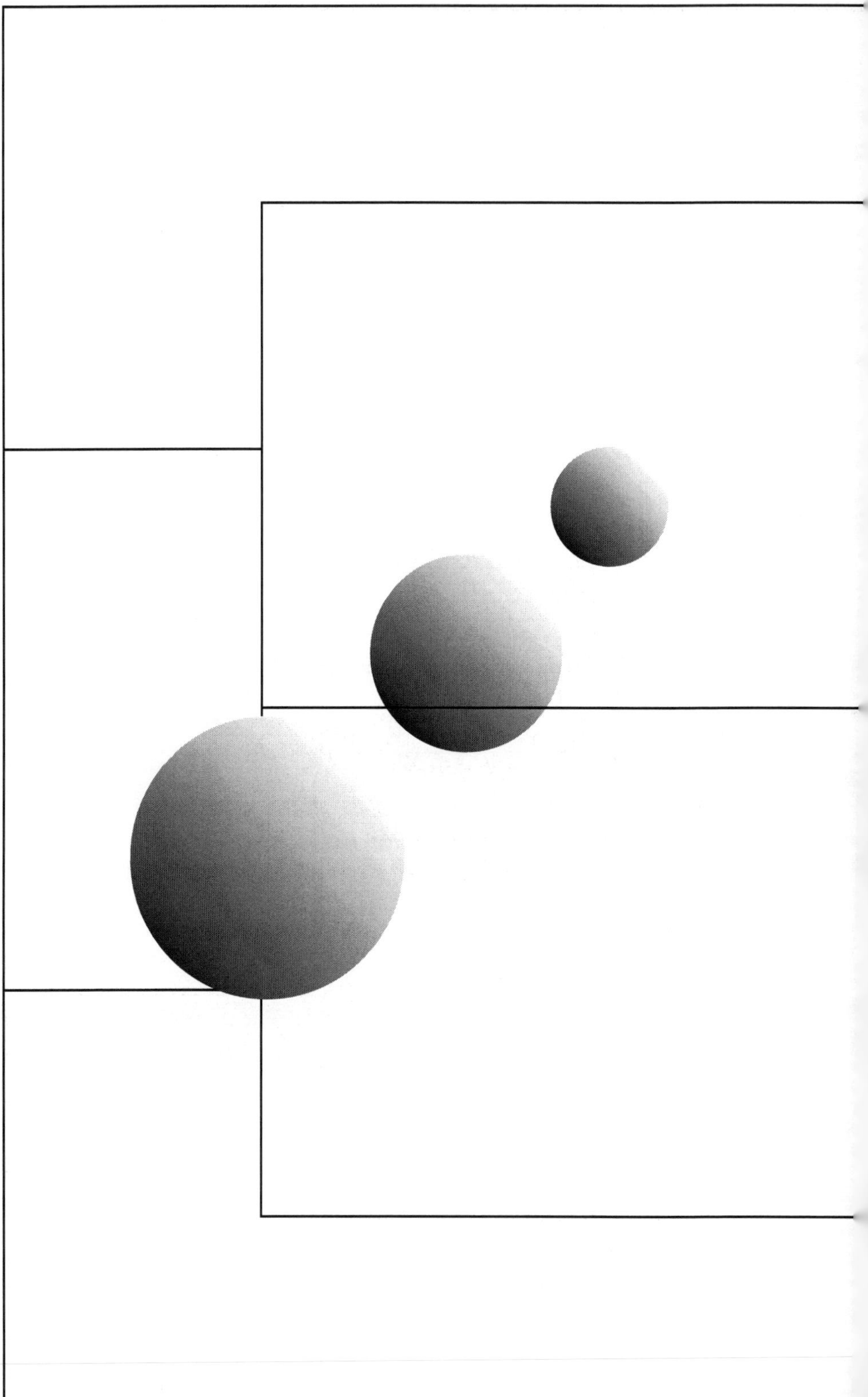

9

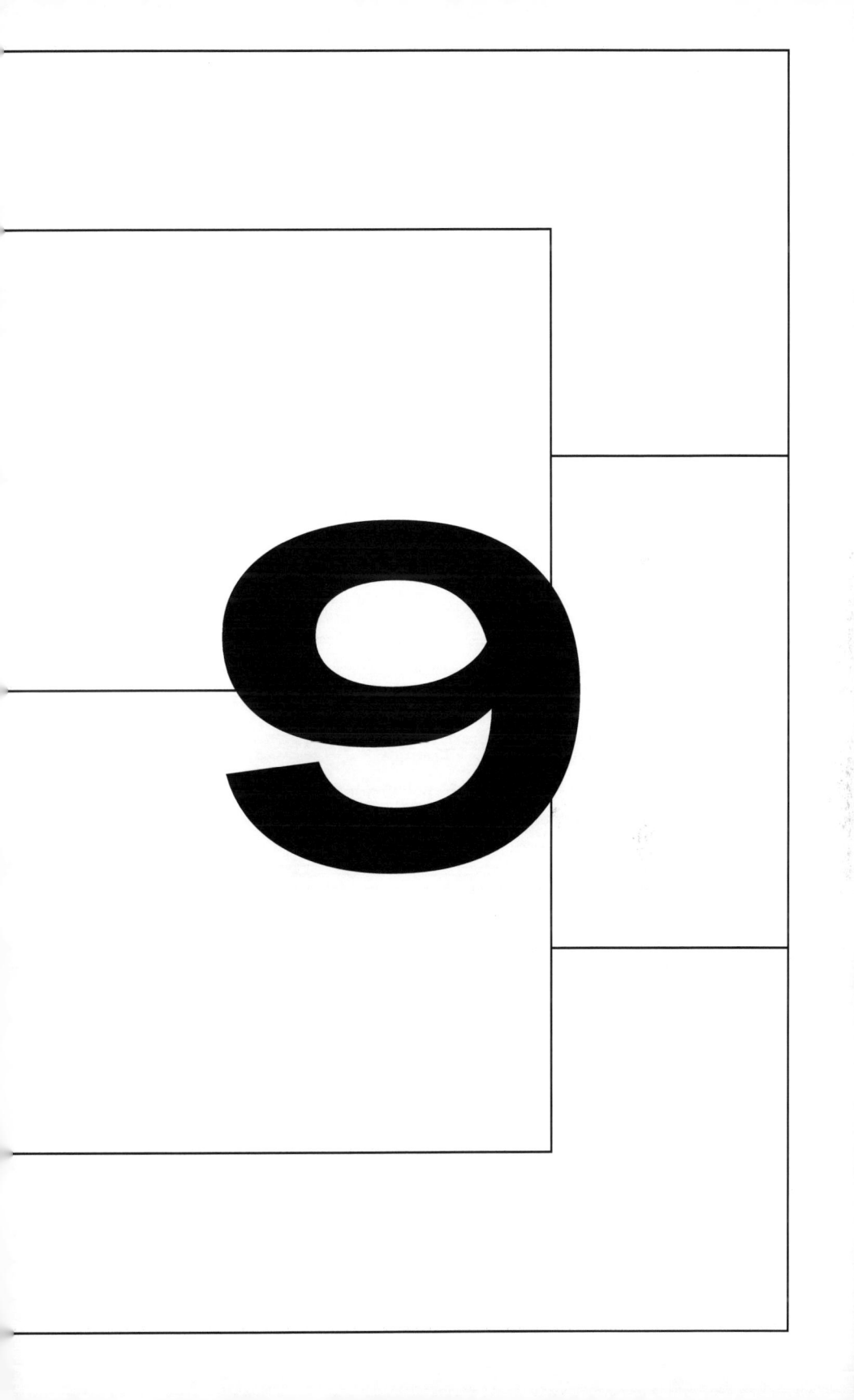

ABOUT RECLAIM

IF YOU ARE READING THIS,
chances are you are starting to rethink what it means to be the Church. Maybe you're surrounded by friends who have zero interest in plugging into anything that whiffs of a church, and you're wondering how to bring Good News to them.

Maybe you're a Church leader with a passion for helping your weary and worn-out friends see that the central message of the bible is "It is finished," not "get it together."

Maybe you grabbed a copy of Reclaim because you've had enough of all the have-tos and how-tos attached to modern ministry, and you have a nagging sense that there is another way.

Whatever your story is, just know that you're not alone, we have been where you are, and we wrote Reclaim for people like you.

The title of this book may be perceived as pridefully suggestive, coming across as a definitive fix-all resource, until you realize that this book is the anti-manual for being the liberated people of God in the world. In an age of religious moralism and institutional metrics, Reclaim seeks to help the global Church retrieve its message of indiscriminate grace and reimagine its ministry within freedom and friendships.

We trust Reclaim will serve you and those with whom you're walking. May it lead to more and more people finding rest in the God who holds them with a love that will not let go.

One last thing. In addition to the book you hold in your hands, we created some additional resources for you. Each Reclaim chapter has a corresponding video of us discussing additional insights and some of our personal "aha" moments. Go to larksite.com/resources to access these free video resources.

larksite.com/resources

RECLAIM
RECLAIM
RECLAIM
RECLAIM
RECLAIM
RECLAIM
RECLAIM
RECLAIM
RECLAIM
RECLAIM
RECLAIM
RECLAIM
RECLAIM

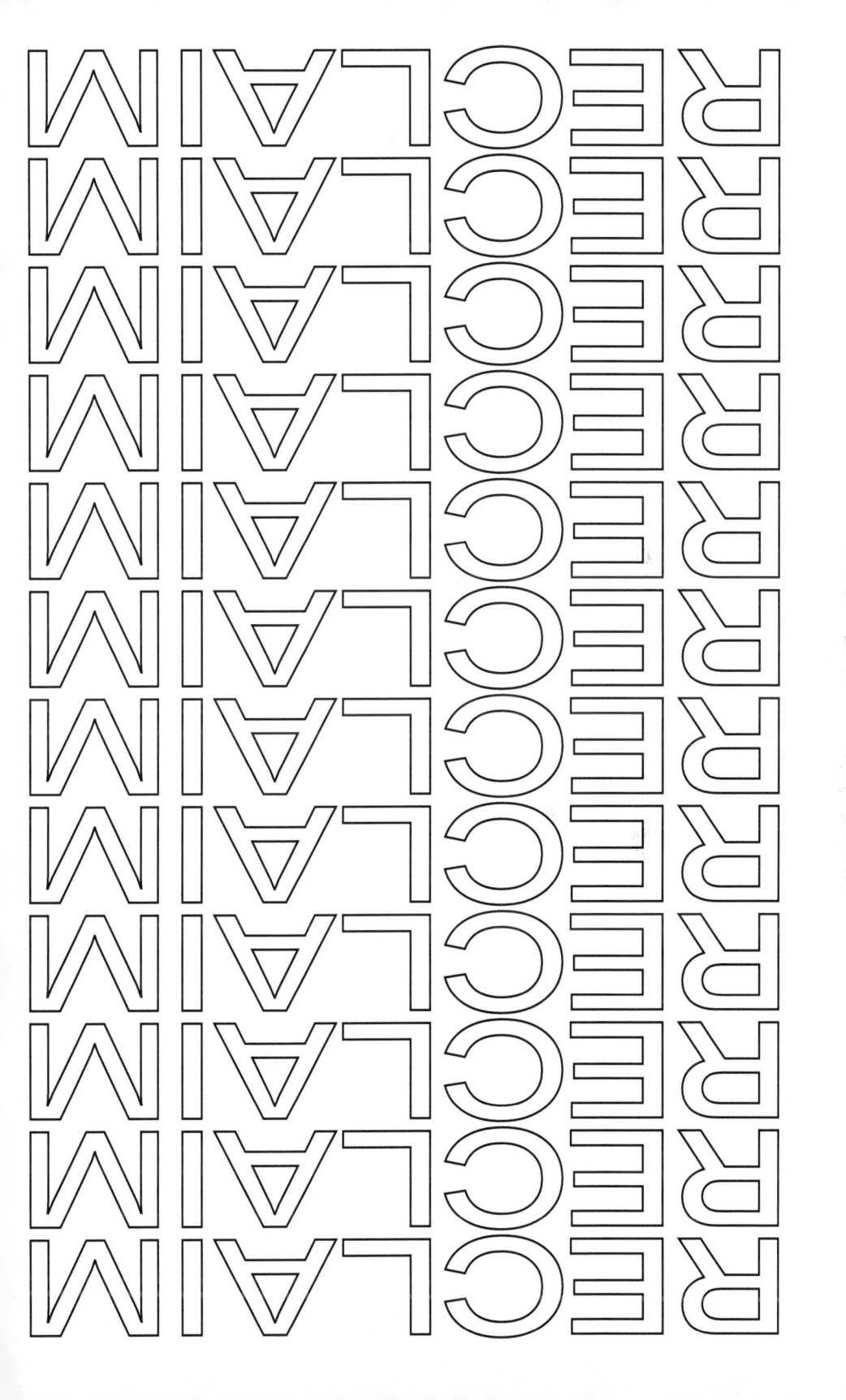

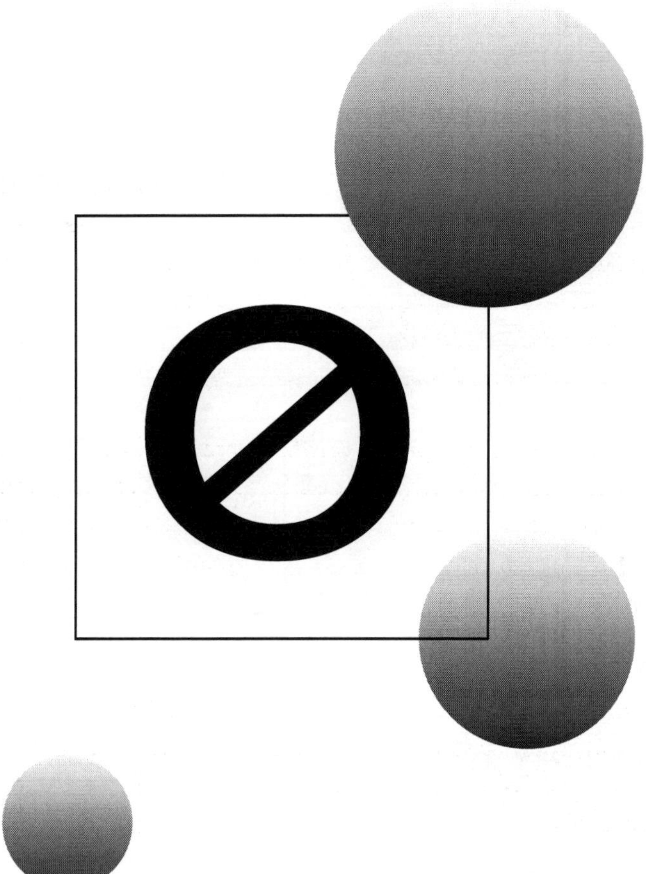

RECLAIM 0

INTRODUCTION

GROWING UP FAST

In the fall of 1997, my life took a significant turn. I had just moved back to the Tampa Bay area to be with a girl named Christa. We had gone to school together since kindergarten, started dating in the 9th grade, and endured a typical roller coaster relationship all throughout high school. But after a time of "moving on," we were finally back together for good. We just hadn't expected to kick off happily ever after with a baby on the way.

With wild and free in my rearview mirror, I needed to find work to support my growing family. Fast. Landing a gig on a freight dock wasn't my first choice, but I couldn't beat the pay. Midnight-to-noon shifts soon taught me that you can dread the very things you're thankful for; and dread it I did. Until I met Tommy.

TOMMY

The first time I saw him, I did a double take. "Mike Tyson? Is that you?" Which was immediately followed by me wondering why I was messing with a guy who looked like Mike Tyson. To my relief, Tommy responded with a chuckle, a smile, and a handshake.

At first, we only interacted occasionally; but I watched as Tommy always greeted everyone with a smile, took the worst work assignments with no complaint, and whistled his way through the day. Tommy was unlike anyone I had ever met. This became even more evident the night I watched him walk into the break room just in time to hear the punchline of a racist joke. Instead of correcting those guys with the skills he acquired as a former hand-to-hand combat instructor in the

Army, he called their racism "sad," told them he would pray for them, and walked away.

Watching from across the room, I dropped my lunch. I had never seen anything like this. Ever. You don't just walk away from a fight. Someone had to inform Tommy of what would happen if he didn't get the respect he was due. Someone had to tell him what would happen if those guys got away with this.

So I caught up with Tommy down the dock to present my case. How he responded is something I will never forget. "Russ, slow your roll. I'm pretty content with who Jesus says I am, which is why I'm not in need of anyone else's approval. Those guys in there, they don't know any better. They are in need of the same grace God has given me. Who am I not to extend it? So I'm going to pray for them. You want to join me?"

I was speechless. I had never heard anything like this before. For the rest of the night, Tommy and I moved freight together as he told me about God's grace. After my shift ended, I went home and told Christa that I had met Jesus and he actually looked a lot like Mike Tyson. She laughed. She also thought I was crazy. Neither one of us had grown up going to church, and our encounters with those who did had left us with little interest in anything coming out of the "God camp."

FREIGHT DOCK DISCIPLE
Despite my bad experiences with people who claimed to be Christians, I suddenly had a desire to learn more about Jesus. So I dug out a little pocket-sized Gideon Bible I kept in an old trunk, brought it to work and showed it to Tommy. He had just been handed the task of unloading a TV trailer—a 53-foot package of misery that required a partner—so he asked me to join him, and we chatted while we worked. To start things off, Tommy gave me a verse to look up. After reading it, I had questions and Tommy shared his insights; then he gave me another verse, and so we went.

During our first break of the night, Tommy invited me to join him and a handful of other guys who were following Jesus. Every night they would get together around a table to catch up, talk about what they were learning, and encourage one another in the good news of Jesus. I had always longed for authentic connection with others. The world is a lonely place for people who are tired of keeping up the facade that they have it all together. A safe, non-judgmental space to be myself as I processed through life was something I had never encountered until that point.

As Tommy and the guys taught me more each day about friendship and freedom in Jesus, I would go home and teach Christa (although I didn't realize that's what I was doing at the time). Through these conversations and a new friendship she had formed with a lamaze coach who knew Jesus, Christa found rest in the cross as well. Our lives would never be the same. And neither would our experience with the Church.

PLUGGING INTO CHRISTENDOM
With the birth of our son, we moved to North Carolina for a new job opportunity. Naturally, we wanted to get connected, so we did what everyone in the Bible Belt instructed us to do: we plugged into a local church. As friendships formed and opportunities surfaced, we started a youth ministry, and I took classes at a local Bible college. Life was good. There was just one problem: what we were being trained to offer in the name of "church" was foreign to what I had experienced on the docks and seen in Scripture. This feeling that something wasn't quite right was confirmed even further when I discovered that none of my neighbors wanted to come to church.

I wasn't alone in feeling this tension back then, and I'm not alone today. Conversations about the steady decline in church attendance and about why 70 percent of society has no interest in attending a church gathering of any kind are just as common now as they were then.

Attempting to make the changes they felt were necessary, the seeker-sensitive movement in the 80s brought modern music to church services and allowed people to wear flip-flops. Amen. In the 90s, the Emergent Church model took shape, allowing everyone to participate in the service and giving leaders the chance to light candles. In the early 2000s, the attractional model took over, bringing with it a new level of production that welcomed fog machines and made room for "preacher sneakers." In 2010, the house church model came to prominence, in which discipleship was the focus. And in 2020 came a new push for social justice to be the primary emphasis of the Church.

On the one hand, I am thankful for the sincerity of these movements. I can point to how each of them has influenced me over the past 20 years as I have planted churches of various styles and launched a network to empower proclaimers of the Good News. But on the other hand, it seems that our ever-changing solutions are never able to adequately address the core question around which the tension revolves: Should the Church function like a hospital for sinners or a schoolhouse for saints?

LEAVING THE CHURCH OF RELIGIOUS MORALISM

In my experience, people view both as worthy pursuits. David Zahl was right when he said that most people feel the Church should be "a place for the wounded to find healing and the healthy to be trained in providing that healing." But I also believe he was correct when he followed that statement by recognizing, "If only the situation were that clear-cut." [1]

I say this because the universal disease of self-reliance—what the Bible refers to as sin—is as real as the lie of independence that comes along with it. In our perpetual push to minimize human nature and maximize human ability, we miss the crisis of capacity Jesus creates when teaching on what should be in our lives, along with the very purpose for which he came into the world.

With the spirit of progress running through humanity's veins, most people view the church as a schoolhouse for saints because it offers them a sense of control. I know I've done this. Seeing transformation as the goal, they present Christianity as morality in action—a religion for the winners who are serious about loving their neighbors as themselves. Believing this to be the will of God, they structure the church to offer everything people need to achieve the ideal self and society.

But Christianity, according to Jesus, is the polar opposite of moralism—a fellowship for the losers who have given up on their ability to truly love God and others as themselves. Believing in Jesus who said the will of God is "that you believe

---

[1] David Zahl, Seculosity (Fortress Press, 2019), page 163.

in the One whom He sent," the Church is freed up to be what God intends: a liberated movement of broken people passing on God's boundless love (Jn 6:29). Portraying ourselves as anything else would be, as Robert Capon puts it, "misleading advertisement." [2]

But that liberated reality won't come easily. Like the most deceptive drug on the market, moralism turns the Church into a religious institution that robs the world of what it needs most: a hospital for sinners. Rachel Held Evans couldn't have painted a better picture of the ER than when she described Jesus' Church like "...a bunch of outcasts and oddballs gathered at a table, not because they are rich or worthy or good, but because they are hungry, because they said yes [to Jesus]. And there's always room for more." [3]

With this vision in mind, Reclaim was born. In it, you will find a journey into the ancient truths that lie in the gap between what is and what could be in the name of "church." From it, you will discover the path you need to help others see what God is truly like so they can rest in what Jesus has really done.

Russ Johnson
Director, Lark

---

[2] Robert Farrar Capon, Kingdom, Grace, Judgment (Grand Rapids, Michicgan, Eerdmans, 2002), pages 115-116.

[3] Rachel Held Evans, Searching for Sunday: Loving, Leaving, and Finding the Church (Nashville, Tennesse, Nelson Books, 2015), page 147.

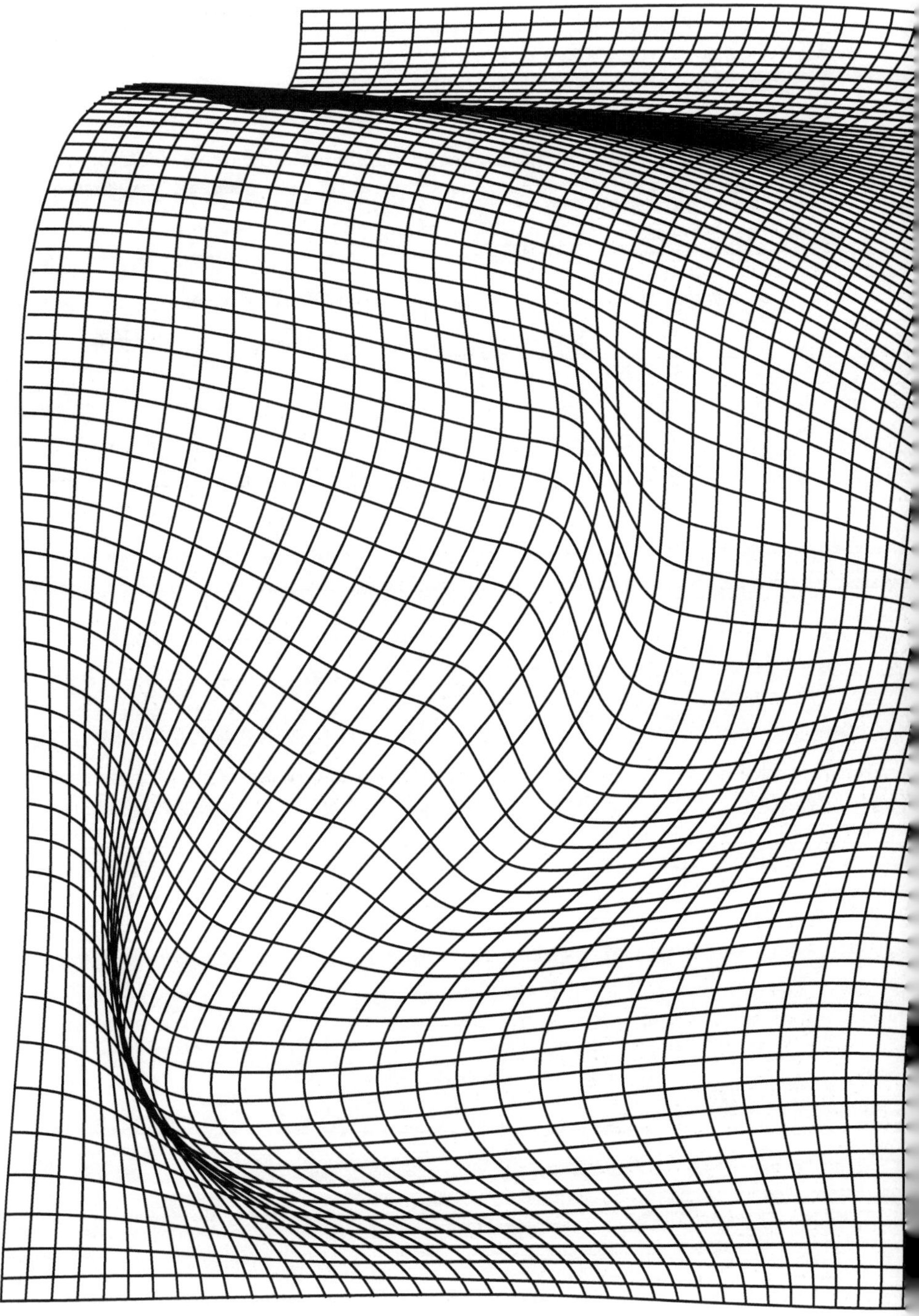

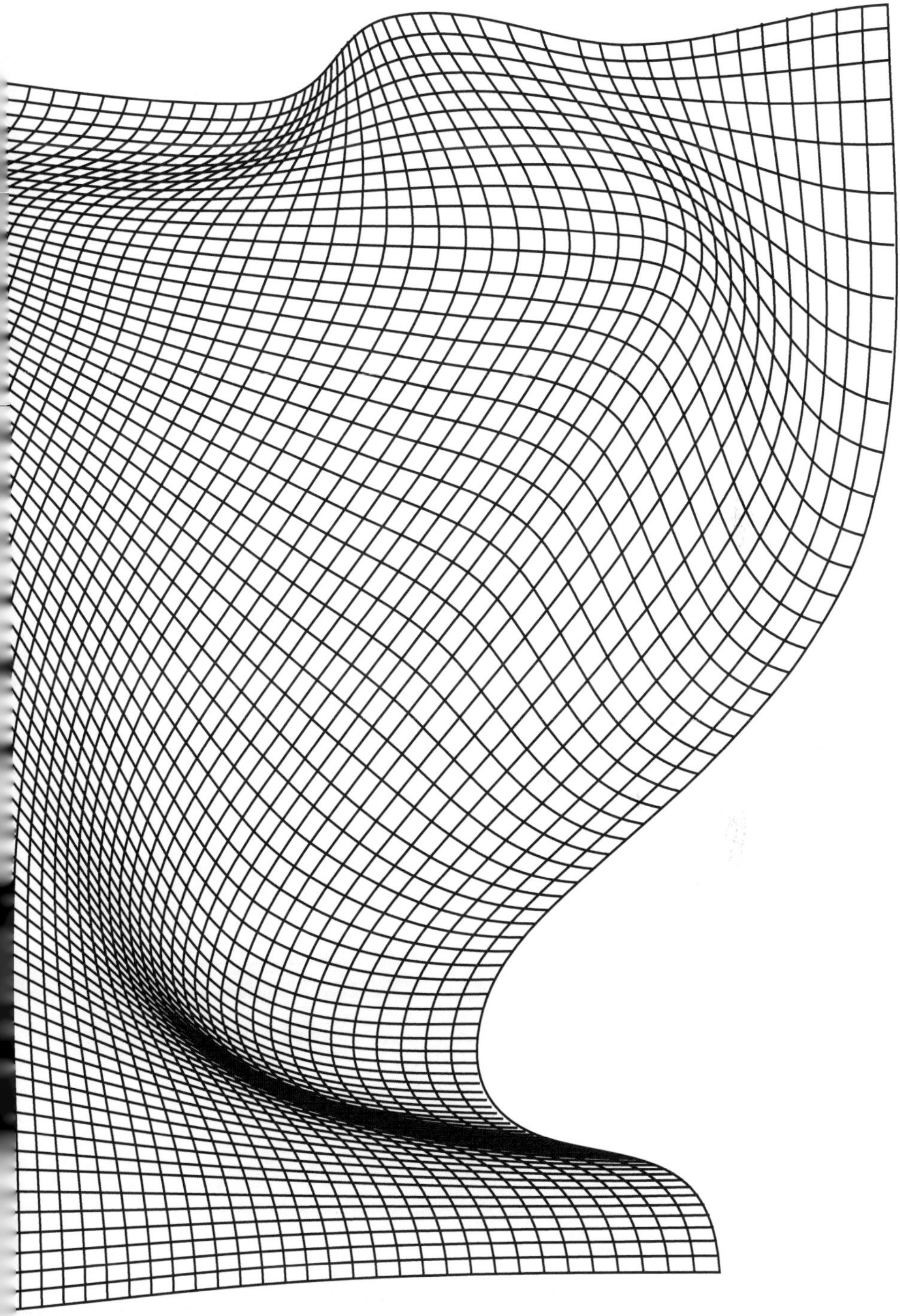

1

RECLAIM 1

JESUS

Jesus. Is there a more controversial name in the entire world? Few names are as emotionally charged, and even fewer carry as much baggage. Jesus is where we begin.

THY KING(DOM) COME

Let's travel to a time before the name Jesus meant much of anything, before wars or religions were ignited in that name. Around 4 BCE, a boy was born to peasant parents in what is now modern-day Palestine. Rumors spread of his mother's controversial insistence that her pregnancy was Divine. The boy grew up as the apprentice to his father, a carpenter. Even with this humble upbringing, this boy, named Jesus, astounded the leaders in the Jewish temple with his understanding of God.

When Jesus was roughly thirty years old, he stepped away from his profession as a carpenter into a different line of work. He started traveling to surrounding Jewish towns, talking about God. Before getting into what he said, we have to understand that the Jewish nation saw itself as the people of God, the ones through whom God would bless all the nations of the world. So basically, Jesus went to the people who believed they were closest to God to tell them about God—that took grit!

Let's just say Jesus failed to ease His way into this new season of work. His first words in Mark's gospel were a stunning announcement: "The Kingdom of God is at hand. Repent and believe this (good news)" (Mk. 1:15).

Jesus was authoritatively telling his fellow Jewish people that the Kingdom of

God had finally arrived. It was the equivalent of saying, "The Kingdom of God has come, and I am the King."

The word "repent" literally means "to turn, to change one's mind." Jesus was telling them to turn from a belief they'd held about God for a very long time—the idea that God was far off and that His Kingdom was inaccessible. Instead, he said, "The Kingdom is a King who has come, and it's standing right in front of you."

Soon after making this stunning proclamation, Jesus began restoring sight to the blind, healing the paralyzed, and casting out demons. Jesus wasn't just telling people the Kingdom had come; he was showing them "the king(dom) was at hand."

"But if it is by the finger of God that I cast out demons, then the Kingdom of God has come upon you." (Lk. 11:20)

SUBVERSIVE & DISRUPTIVE

Saying and doing things like this dramatically upsets the status quo. And who has the most to lose when the status quo is upset? That's right. Those in power. Specifically, religious and political power.

Jesus was subverting the powers of his day. He was a threat to the carefully maintained system that kept people in line—a system that ensured they remained dependent on those in power. To add insult to authoritative injury, Jesus gathered 12 guys who were sure to be picked last in rabbinical kickball and was soon sending them to do the same things he was doing.

If there was one thing the religious conservatives (the Pharisees) and the religious liberals (the Sadducees) could agree on, it was that Jesus needed to be stopped. In the minds of these opposing political and religious leaders, Jesus was attempting to start a revolution, and he had to be stopped.

Commoners, however, wanted a revolution. They were tired of the injustice served to them by the Romans and the religious leaders. So they chose Jesus. They sat at his feet and wrapped themselves around his words. Even the discarded and despised of Jesus' day shared meals with him and were drawn into the conversation.

Jesus wasn't turning out to be a fad like some had expected. He was gaining popularity, and drastic measures needed to be taken to silence him. After many failed attempts to trip Jesus up publicly, those who opposed him found someone in his inner circle they could bribe — Judas. The infamous traitor handed Jesus over to the Roman authorities for the modern equivalent of roughly four hundred dollars. Jesus was arrested on the grounds of being an insurgent and a heretic. His message had grown increasingly bolder to the point of declaring himself one with God: "Whoever has seen Me has seen the Father" (Jn. 14:9).

Although the official courts did not find any evidence to convict him, those who hated Jesus relentlessly accused him. They demanded his execution. In an effort to assuage social unrest, the Roman government decided to grant the mob's request—an innocent man was sentenced to death.

Jesus—who had an affinity for controversy and was known for miraculous healings and the multiplying of food—was killed like a common criminal by crucifixion (the Roman punishment for those who opposed the empire). After his death, Jesus was laid in a tomb with a massive stone in place to block its entrance. Roman guards were stationed to guard it with their very lives. They were to protect the tomb at all costs. To fail at this assignment was to be put to death.

The movement that had started to gain momentum around the person of Jesus seemed to die with him. None were more shocked and despondent than his followers, who immediately retreated into hiding. This was the exact response Jesus' enemies desired and expected.

However, a few days later, his formerly scattered and afraid followers began running around claiming to have seen Jesus alive and well. The tomb was undeniably empty—and the Scriptures, as well as extra-biblical sources of both Roman and Jewish origin, record that more than five hundred people saw him alive.

Jesus' closest followers swore to the truth of his resurrection, and this eventually led to all of their deaths. Yet no matter how many were killed, the message was unstoppable. This is the story of Jesus. This is the Good News.

LIFE OUTSIDE OF JESUS IS A MYTH

When asked, "Who is Jesus?" we begin with the historical narrative. This discussion, however, is far from over because if this story is true, then the ramifications are paramount. If this story is true, then Jesus is the key to glorious things like hope, meaning, forgiveness, joy, purpose, and life itself. If this story is true, then the kingdom of God is near and accessible to the least, last, and lost among us. If this story is true, Jesus is our creator, sustainer, and reconciler as declared in Colossians 1:15-20.

> He is the image of the invisible God, the firstborn of *all* creation. For by him *all* things were created, in heaven and on earth, visible and invisible, whether thrones or dominions or rulers or authorities — *all* things were created through him and for him. And he is before *all* things, and in him, *all* things hold together. And he is the head of the body, the church. He is the beginning, the firstborn from the dead, that in *everything* he might be preeminent. For in him *all* the fullness of God was pleased to dwell, and through him to reconcile to himself *all* things, whether on earth or in heaven, making peace by the blood of his cross. (emphasis ours)

Everything in existence—past, present, and future—was and is created by Jesus, through Jesus, and for Jesus. By his mere desire, the entire universe was created and is sustained.

In this passage, Paul is saying the same thing John said of Jesus in the first words of his gospel: "In the beginning was the Word, and the Word was with God, and the Word was God. He was in the beginning with God. *All things were made through him, and without him was not anything made that was made. In him was life, and the life was the light of men*" (John 1:1-4, emphasis ours).

Paul is also saying the same thing Jesus said of himself: "I am the way, the truth, and *the life...*" (John 14:6a, emphasis ours).

There is no escaping his presence; there is no hiding from his sight. He is relentless in his passionate pursuit of people. He is steadfast in his patience with this world. Not only is forgiveness found in Christ, but also life! He is the life and the light of the whole world!

Consider for a moment what this means for those who don't yet believe in Jesus. For the longest time, I (Tony) viewed my friends, family, and neighbors who didn't trust Jesus through the lens of separation and distance from God. I would frequently refer to people who didn't believe as those who are "far from God."

While we should maintain that no one has a relationship with God or lives in the joy of who he is and what he has done apart from faith, we should also point out that he created and sustains all of human life regardless of one's beliefs.

Paul essentially said the same thing when he addressed an assembly of unbelieving intellectuals and philosophers, saying, "... [God] is actually not far from each one of us, for in [Jesus] we *all* live and move and have our being" (Acts 17:27b-28a, emphasis ours). How, for so long, did I maintain that Jesus separated himself from my neighbors, when in reality he is near to them and is their very life, moment by moment?

ALL THINGS ARE RECONCILED

Looking back at Colossians 1, we want to point out one essential and profound truth.

If we can agree with Scripture to say: all creation takes a backseat to Jesus, the firstborn (v.15); all things were created by Jesus and for Jesus (v.16); all things came after the eternal Jesus (v.17a); all things are held together by Jesus (v.17b); and all the fullness of God dwelt in Jesus (v.19), then we must also affirm verse 20 in saying that "all things," in heaven and on earth, are *already* reconciled, and peace has already been made across the cosmos (heaven and earth).

The beauty of Paul announcing this cosmic reconciliation right after five other universal cosmic realities is that we don't really have to wonder, "Does all really mean all?"

Why is this difficult to grasp and why is it so important?

It's difficult to grasp because this reconciliation and peace are not often felt or seen around the world, around the corner, or perhaps even around our own homes. In fact, sometimes a lack of reconciliation and peace seems to be the only thing we can see. And yet, despite our inability to detect this reconciling peace among those in the world, the more important reality is what God, in Jesus, has accomplished on behalf of the world.

It's important to grasp this because it's what makes the news of the cross actual good news, not just potential good news. When one awakens to the reconciling King known as Jesus, they awaken to a reality already fixed in regards to their very existence.

Regardless of the posture and position of the world toward God—the more important thing to consider is the reality of God's posture and position toward the world. For some, Jesus reconciling the world in a single act, independent of anyone's opinion on the matter—whether acceptance or rejection—is hard to accept because it feels like Universalism. Universalism asserts that EVERYONE will be saved. Instead, we're holding these statements are true, regardless of whether someone is saved or not: It is true that everyone finds their very existence in Jesus who is "life" (Jn 14:6); it is also true that Jesus has reconciled "all things" (Col 1:20).

THE KING(DOM) IS EVERYWHERE

Seeing Jesus as a present, accessible, sustaining, and reconciling King helps us make sense of his parables about the permeating presence of the kingdom in the world. In Luke 8:1-15, Jesus says the kingdom of God is like a "sower who went out to sow" seed everywhere. Some seeds fell on the path and were devoured by birds, some on rocky ground that allowed for no root to form, some fell among thorns that choked them out, and some on good soil that produced grain.

After Jesus shares this parable, the disciples come to him with some questions (Luke 8:9 and Mark 4:10-13). Jesus provides them with a seemingly straightforward explanation, leading us to wonder: Why were they so confused in the first place? Yet we need to be mindful of our own fallibility when approaching Scriptures like this one. It's tempting to assume that the disciples were slow on the uptake based on their need for clarification on such a simple story. However, based on the many modern interpretations of this parable, we're confident a good number of us would've been left scratching our heads as well.

We've all heard sermons and witnessed discipleship models that imagine the Church picking up where Jesus left off as the sower, going to the ends of the earth to spread the word of God in places where it isn't yet present or believed. But are we the sowers here? Are our feeble attempts to share Jesus the seed—the "word of God?" (Luke 8:11)

Instead of placing the Church at the center of this parable and interpreting the "word of God" as a mission trip to a third world country, we might be on firmer ground by interpreting Scripture with Scripture. In doing so, we understand the "word" in light of a passage we looked at earlier: "In the beginning was the Word, and the Word was with God, and the Word was God. All things were made through him, and without him was not anything made that was made. ... And the Word became flesh and dwelt among us" (Jn 1:1-3; 14, emphasis ours).

Can you see it now? The Father, not the Church, must be the sender/sower. He "sent" his Son into the world (1 Jn. 4:14). Jesus is the Word. He is the seed lavishly sown into every nook and cranny of the world—even the not-so-nice places like among weeds and on hardened paths.

What does this mean? His reconciling presence has already been sown throughout every place in the cosmos. There isn't a single square inch of the world where the Word won't be present and waiting for us—even those who desire to carry this Good News wherever they go.

This changes everything.

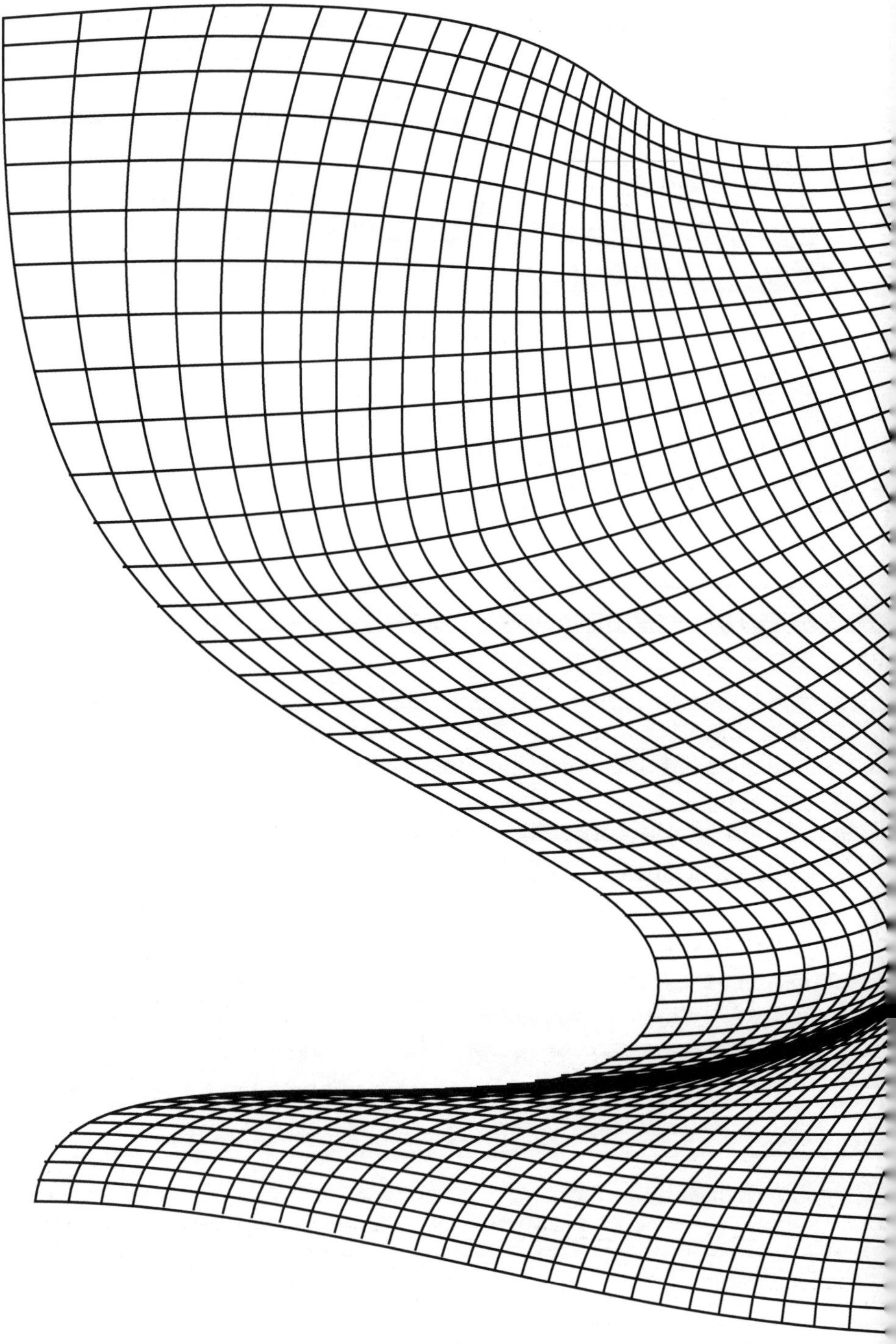

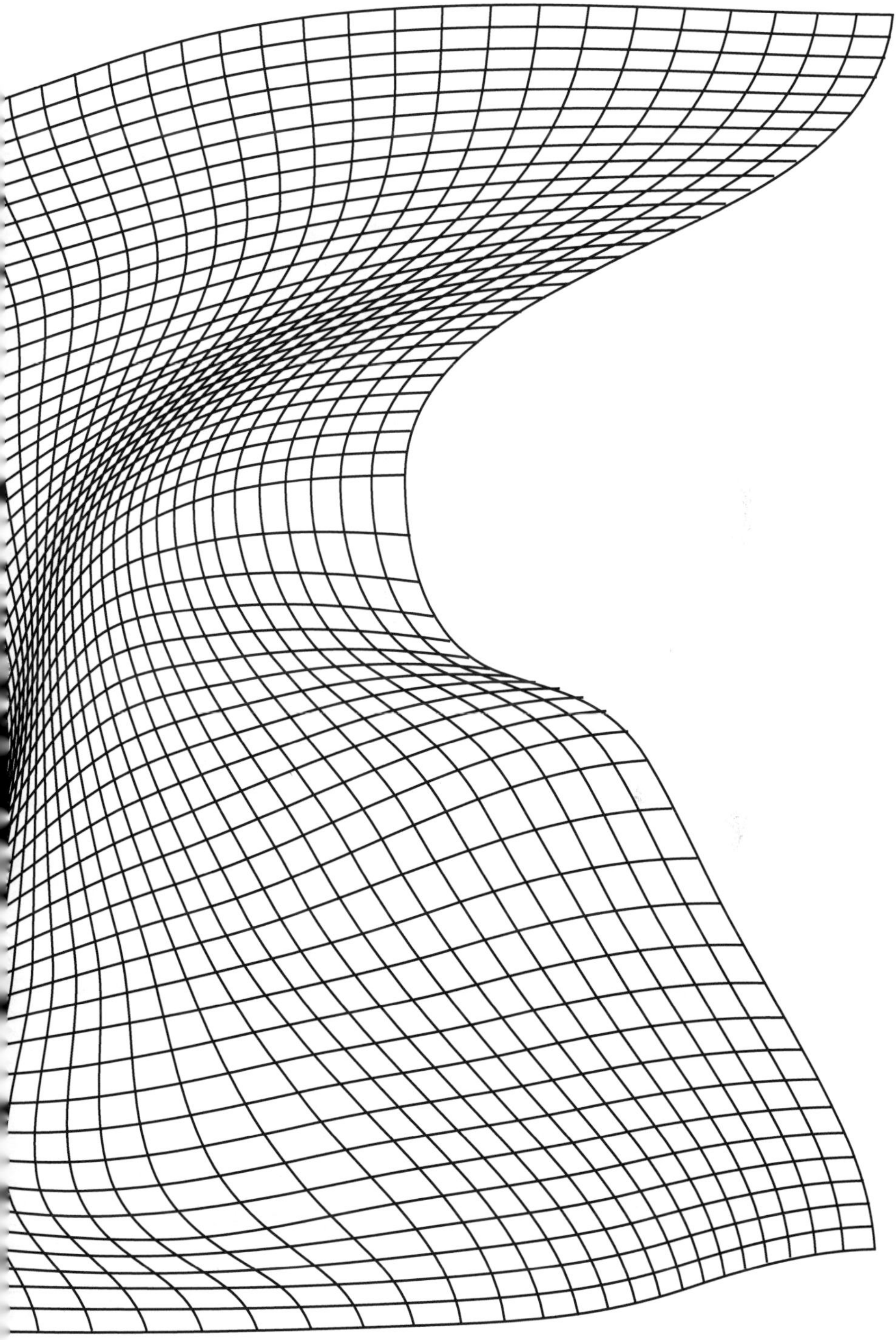

2

RECLAIM 2

CROSS

In the words of an American punk rock band from Scranton, Pennsylvania, "There's so much to be sad about these days."

Regardless of your vantage point, you don't have to look any further than your Twitter feed or local news to see that our world is messed up. Story after story, it's hard to watch without feeling discouraged.

Maybe the dysfunction of this world (and perhaps even some of the dysfunction in your own life) has you genuinely longing for change and cultural transformation. Maybe your desire is for the broken things in society and in your life to be made right. Perhaps you long for evil to be dealt with and done away with for good. If that's you, then you have a whole lot in common with those who awaited the coming King whom God had promised in the Old Testament.

ISO: WONDER-WORKING MESSIAH W/ MILITARY EXPERIENCE

These believers longed for the coming of the Messiah and held to Scriptures like Isaiah 9:6-7:

> For a child has been born for us, a son is given to us; authority rests upon his shoulders; and he is named Wonderful Counselor, Mighty God, Everlasting Father, Prince of Peace. His authority shall grow continually, and there shall be endless peace for the throne of David and his kingdom. He will establish and uphold it with justice and with righteousness from this time onward and forevermore.

After prolonged years of waiting, this promised Son finally came. It was God himself who eventually showed up in the person of Jesus and announced, "The kingdom of God is at hand" (Mk. 1:14-15).

"Finally!" they thought. "Game on! God has come to rescue us from Rome's oppression and make the world straighten up and fly right."

Even John the Baptist, whose mission in life was to prepare the way for the Messiah, rejoiced at his coming by telling people that Jesus had come to separate the good from the bad and to judge with fire (Matt. 3:11-12). They couldn't wait to get back to the way it was under King David: an independent and free nation with a powerful military.

[didn't fit the expectation]

But when Jesus came onto the scene, none of those things appeared to happen. Jesus seemed to be content restoring sight to the blind, healing those born lame, cleansing lepers, raising the dead, and preaching good news to all. At first, it appeared that Jesus was bringing this kingdom using the power of miracles. Early in his ministry, it seemed like he healed everyone he came across. Demons and diseases were no match for him. This is what drew the crowds and made him famous. News of this Miracle Worker even made its way to Herod the Great (Mk. 6:14).

This was the kind of power people craved (and still do). Perhaps you think Jesus could have fixed our broken world and the people within it by setting up a miracle shop at the main intersection between Judea and Galilee. He could book healing appointments back-to-back every day for the rest of his life. A toothache cured at 9:00 in the morning. A broken finger at 9:15. A limp leg healed at 9:30 and sight restored at 10:00. Sounds good until you realize that:

1. There wouldn't be enough time in the day to see everyone
2. After these healings, more issues of the flesh would inevitably arise (even those raised from the dead inevitably die again).
3. By emphasizing signs and wonders, people would miss the essence of their actual need: reconciliation. *[restoration of relations — the action of making a view or belief compatable w/ another]*

Eventually, Jesus began withdrawing from the crowds who sought him only for what he could give them, and before long, the miracles almost ceased altogether.

All of this non-intervention left John the Baptist (who was in prison at that time) doubting if Jesus was really the One from God who'd get the job done. He even sent messengers to Jesus asking if he should begin looking for another Messiah (Matt. 11:2-6). Those wanting a swift cleansing of the world ended up disappointed.

At the end of all Jesus' traveling, teaching, miracles, and subsequent death and resurrection, he simply disappeared—literally ascending into Heaven—seemingly leaving behind no kingdom to provide rescue or reform for the world.

RIGHT-HANDED VS. LEFT-HANDED POWER

Jesus was perfectly capable of opening the proverbial "can" on all the world's evil. So why the delay? Why not wipe out every single enemy, take your rightful place as King, and fill the world with tangible righteousness? The answer is found in what the famous 16th century German theologian Martin Luther described as "left-handed power."

Right-handed power gets things done directly. It is the power of numbers, size, and military strength. It is the power of hierarchy, force, money, grandeur, and success. Left-handed power, on the other hand, is very different. Luther described it as "paradoxical power." In fact, it doesn't look like power at all. Instead, it seems more like weak, shameful losing. It is the power of love, forgiveness, and sacrificial service. And yet, Luther argues, it is the most powerful force in the world.

Right-handed power is the way of the world. It's how it operates and gets things done, and it is very effective. Yet it becomes somewhat ineffective if you care more about maintaining a relationship than achieving a specific result.

The answer to Jesus' delay in defeating evil, which ultimately turned out to be for our good, is found in the use of left-handed power. Jesus certainly could have set things right and destroyed all those who opposed him but more important to Jesus was restoring relationships—even with sinners (us). He used this paradoxical form of power to win us back, instead of wiping us out. When you consider how he did this—dying on a cross—it's a remarkably odd way of demonstrating power, isn't it?

The cross was the instrument of death chosen by the Romans to declare their victory over someone in the most humiliating and painful of ways. If John the Baptist had not been beheaded earlier in prison, he would have been seriously doubting Jesus' messiahship at that point. In John's mind, kings and messiahs don't lose, and they most certainly don't die.

JESUS KNEW HIS MISSION

During the three years Jesus spent with his disciples, he spoke plainly, honestly, and openly about why he had come into this world. Like most people bent toward the winner's circle (people like us), the disciples didn't understand or believe Jesus' announcement. Matthew, one of Jesus' disciples, recorded, "From that time Jesus began to show his disciples that he must go to Jerusalem and suffer many things... and be killed, and on the third day be raised" (Matt. 16:21).

It seems Jesus was familiar with the job description given to him before his birth (Matt. 1:21). He wasn't shy about why he had come or cryptic about his mission. He said himself, "For even the Son of Man came not to be served but to serve, and to give his life as a ransom for many" (Mk. 10:45).

While Jesus plainly told those closest to him that his life would end in Jerusalem, it never really sunk in for them. And let's not forget the time Peter reprimanded Jesus for talking about dying (Matt. 16:22). His inner circle still had their hearts set on Jesus being the prototypical action hero who would bring swift judgment on God's enemies. Surely, there would be a heap of bodies and a whole lot of blood by the time he was done with them (aka, right-handed power).

But in the end, it was Jesus' body that was horrendously disfigured. It was his blood that was shed. Instead of judgment being brought on God's enemies, it was brought on God's Son. What kind of power is that?

On the surface, God's intervention in this world through Christ seemed like non-intervention. What was God doing?! Why was he losing?! Why was he dying?! The Apostle Peter told us why when he explained that "... Christ also suffered once for sins, the righteous for the unrighteous, that he might bring us to God..." (1 Pet. 3:18).

In Jesus' death, we come to discover the heart of God toward the losers of this world (me and you) who have done a number on his creation: the restoration of a relationship—or as we pointed out in Reclaim 1, reconciliation.

GOOD NEWS: IT IS FINISHED

For some of us, this might seem like an ineffective way to fix the world. As fans of a more direct approach, we would have preferred the Messiah to arrive with a thorough clean-up operation. But instead of dealing with the world using military tactics, he chose to set a table for it.

The mission of Jesus was not to fix the Roman Empire. It wasn't his mission to disciple enough people so they could, in turn, disciple enough people to fix Rome and then the rest of the world. His mission wasn't even to live a life of love and service that, if emulated by others, would fix the world. While our hearts long for this world to be fully healed and advocate for things like discipleship and love, we must grapple with the plain truth that Jesus' mission was to die. This simple reality is not only good news, it's the best news this world has ever known.

On the cross, Jesus announced that his Father's dealings with the sin problem of this world are "FINISHED" (Jn. 19:28-30). Jesus' words of assurance that, "It is finished," mean just that. Everything that ever needed to be done or ever would need to be done by us to be reconciled to God has been done. Neither you nor anyone else can mess up or undo this work because... well, it's finished.

It's why we refer to the sufferings of Jesus as good news. It happened. The historical nature of it is what makes it news. The work of Jesus was never meant to be an inspirational model for you to adopt and apply to your life. It was indeed a single act of love that reconciled the cosmos (Col. 1:20). It was a "left-handed" act so subversively powerful that evil itself could not reverse it. It was a "left-handed" act so powerful that no one will ever need to do a single religious act—or lift a religious finger—again to live in the freedom found in our King.

The good news for the broken (the only kind of people there are) is that God has never asked us to clean ourselves up or reach a certain level of righteousness before taking a seat at his table. Instead, he does for us (in Christ) what we could never do for ourselves. He provides us with everything needed to live and dwell in fellowship with him. "For our sake, he made him to be sin who knew no sin, so that in him we might become the righteousness of God" (2 Cor. 5:21, see also Rom. 4:4-5).

In what Luther called "The Great Exchange," our sin was placed on Christ and, by faith, the very righteousness and perfection of Jesus are placed on us. This is the ultimate leveling of all playing fields. In Christ, there's no room for boasting (Rom. 3:27-28).

Tim Keller says it well: "The prostitute and king, male and female, Jew and Gentile, one race and another race, moral and immoral—all sit down as equals. Equally sinful and lost, equally accepted and loved."[1]

ADVANCING THE KINGDOM?

As we look to the Scriptures through this lens, we learn that Jesus did bring a kingdom. It wasn't a kingdom of right-handed power built with force and strength. Instead, it's built on the left-handed power of a King who descended from his throne to die for the rebels of his kingdom so that they could live.

When we view the King and his kingdom through this lens, we have to ask where all the talk of "ushering in" the kingdom came from? All the mission conference rallying cries, passionate sermons, and church marketing using this language have led to the idea that somehow you and I are tasked with "advancing" the kingdom like some sort of holy football team. We've even adopted phrases like "gaining kingdom ground" and "a kingdom win." The question begs to be asked, how can we advance a kingdom that has already been sown throughout the whole world?

This brief look into the Scriptures shows us that the kingdom is not something we build or advance, but a King who has announced, "It is finished." Through him, the kingdom presently exists as an "unshakable" reality. Indeed, it is Someone we simply "receive" (Heb. 12:27-28).

Understanding this allows us to move from a mindset of building to resting

---

1 Timothy Keller, Hidden Christmas, (New York, New York, Viking, 2016), page 33.

while looking for opportunities to share the good news of the King, who has invited us all into a celebration of his finished work.

After all, loving my neighbor as a guest at the table instead of as a general contractor of a missional project actually frees me up to walk with them over the long haul.

THE KING OF KINGDOM ETHICS

Making a big deal out of the three words "it is finished" will often sound an alarm in the mind of anyone who has migrated from churches that don't give equal attention to the social needs of society as they do the individual aspects of salvation. If that's you, we want to share a quick word.

We share in your heart for your neighborhoods, cities, states, and the world. In fact, the Reclaim journey is designed to help you live into a life of love among your neighbors—including the disconnected and disenfranchised. However, we've found some aspects of the gospel focused on social justice to be quite limiting in this pursuit, just as it is limiting to focus only on the individual aspects.

First, if our heart is to love those disregarded in society because of their age, ethnicity, economic status, geography, gender, orientation and so on, then we must remind ourselves that these acts of love are the fruit of the King—they are not the kingdom itself. Our love can point to the King who loves the oppressed and is at work in us, but these acts are limited and temporary because they are dependent upon our being alive, in good health, and having time and a means of income to be generous. The kingdom of God, however, is unlike our love. The love of the King is unfailing and eternal; our love is frail and temporal. This is why Jesus never writes us in as the main character in his parables. All of the parables Jesus tells about the kingdom are stories, not about what we can do, but about what God is like despite what anyone does or doesn't do.

To care for people in this temporary life is good and beautiful. But to invite people into the life of the King who will never leave them transcends this temporal good. Far from an either/or position, this is a both/and position with a recognition that the gift-Giver is better than the gift itself.

Second, while confronting the injustices we see around us and helping the victims, we can subtly begin communicating, "Only victims are welcome here." This emphasis ignores the actual problem both parties have in common: the disease of self-reliance (i.e. sin) presents false solutions that never offer a cure and provides no relief to the other sinners in the equation—those victimizing people.

We need to remind ourselves that Jesus invited the oppressed and the oppressors to the table. Followers of Jesus included wealthy tax collectors (Matthew) and the poor, exploited slave girls (Acts 16:16-18) and Roman soldiers (Mk. 15:39), the religiously oppressed (Mt. 11:28) and religious oppressors (Jn. 19:39). There was even a disciple of Jesus (one of the twelve closest to him) that was a Jewish political terrorist named Simon, who belonged to a group called "the Zealots." While the joy of the gospel is that God delights to extend grace and forgiveness to us and to those we love, the offense of the gospel is that God also delights to do the same for our enemies.

Lastly, it's easy to trade environments centered on performance and personal morality for environments focused on social involvement. Instead of the pressure to maintain acceptable levels of personal sanctification through spiritual disciplines, people are expected to be growing in wokeness, empathy, and involvement. The danger here is in how both camps introduce a conditionality to belonging that is foreign to the unconditional belonging found in Jesus. We've seen from personal experience how this kind of conditionality leads to posturing and policing one another when it comes to behaviors and beliefs. This kind of culture never leads to real change and love, only acquiescence and practice rooted in pressure.

The real loss on both sides is that we continue to perpetuate the stereotype of the Church as a place of performance and challenge instead of a place of relief and comfort to an already exhausted world—the reason why most are disinterested in the Church in the first place.

In practice, Christianity (in both its personal and social forms) becomes a means to the earthly end of fixing ourselves and the world around us. We understand the desire we all have to bring about the ideal life for ourselves and our neighbors in the here and now; but we have to remind ourselves of how God went about "fixing" the world. He bore all of our sin in his death and raised all of humanity at once. The One who cares infinitely more about social injustice and individual inconsistencies chose to die to forgive rather than to fix. There's something important for all of us to consider in this seemingly foolish method of left-handed power.

The Kingdom ethic above all Kingdom ethics is that the King came to die for the rebels, the religious, oppressors, and oppressed alike (Jn. 15:13).

His death and resurrection for us is the only means we have to experience the love and unity we long to walk in. The crucified Son was God's answer to every personal and global issue. Jesus said that his mission—the one not even his disciples grasped while he walked the earth with them—was to die. The salvation of the world came through the death of its King, and by him alone "all things" are made right, because only by him are they made "new" (Rev. 21).

In Jesus, we're free to join any people, pocket, or place in the world without judging those who do, don't or do otherwise. We can lead conversations on the Scriptures or serve soup or both. The question is, will we rest in this "finished" work of Jesus and relate this Good News to those we love? Or will we present to them that something else is still needed to change the world?

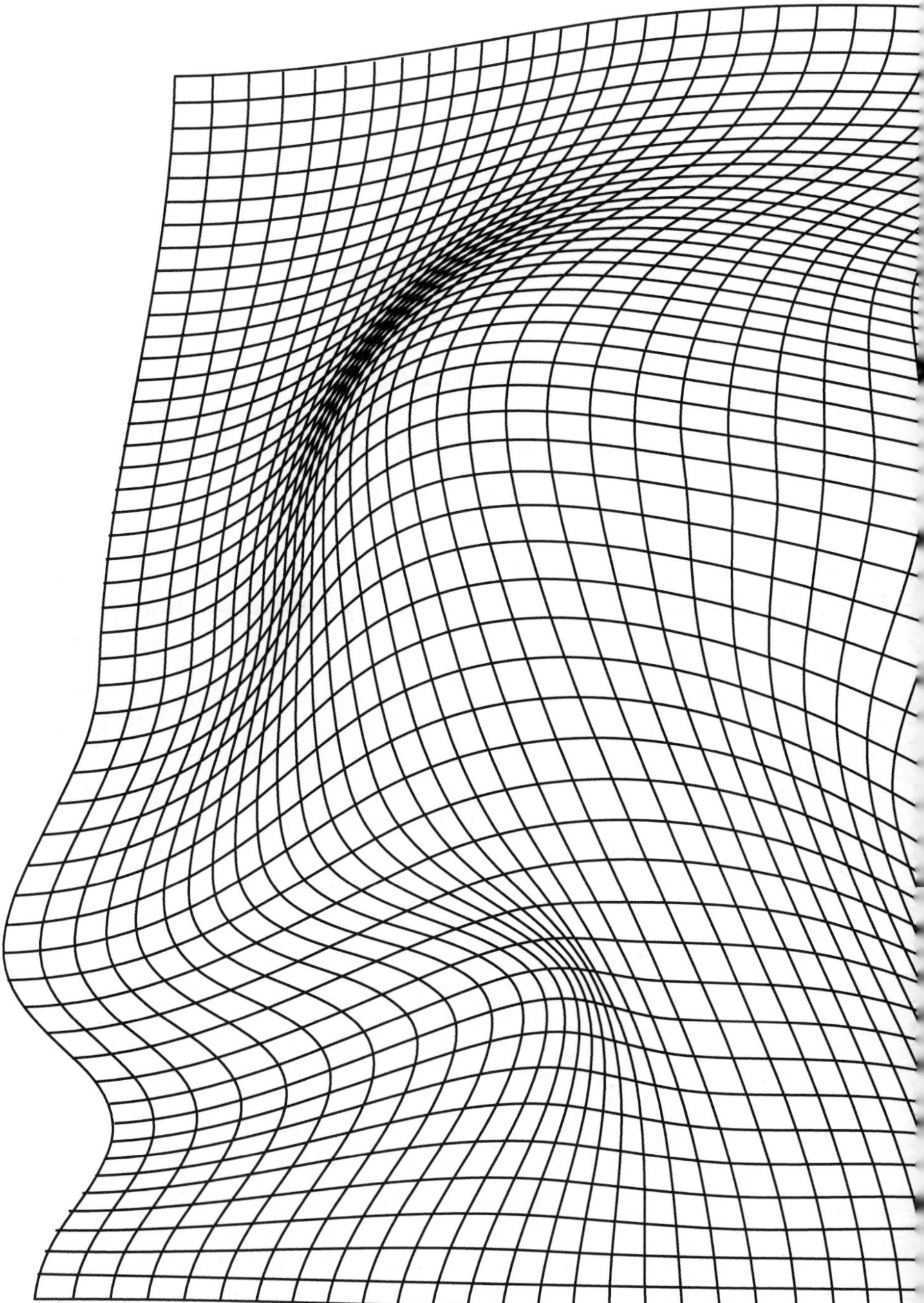

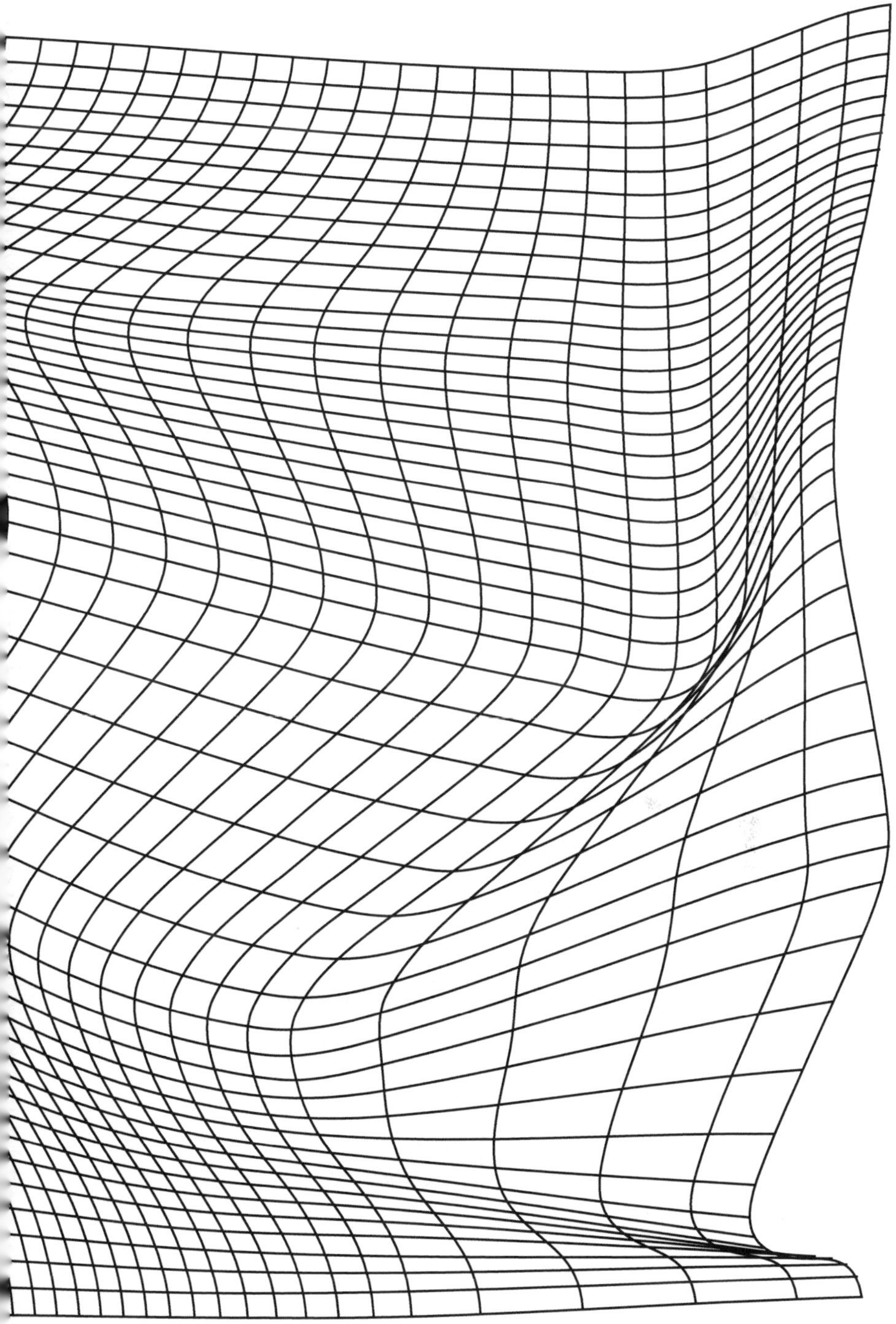

3

RECLAIM 3

TRUST

"I'm tired, man. I can't keep up with everything I'm supposed to think, value, say, not say, do, not do, who I'm supposed to be friends with, who I need to cancel, the list goes on. One minute it's sucking the life out of me, and the next minute I find myself acting no different than the legalistic church I walked away from. They said this was the 'real movement of Jesus,' but it's just the same culture with different language about God. What do I do?"

As I (Russ) listened to an old friend describe his church experience and share his heart over the phone, I was burdened for him but growing frustrated. I can point to a number of people, stories, and conversations over the years that have sounded very similar to this. Regardless of the denomination, theological emphasis, cultural stance, or worship style, my friend's words show the effects of the most deceptive drug in the world: religious moralism. Religious moralism is the belief that we can eventually make ourselves right(eous) in God's eyes through what we think, say, and do in this life.

Will Stor described the "perfectionism" religion offers well when he said that people everywhere are literally "suffering and dying under the torture of the fantasy self they're failing to become." And, sadly, the Church of Jesus is rarely any different.

I've observed leader-types smothering people with the project of self-justification and a misunderstanding of self-actualization. All in Jesus' name. While we long for the good life, we're selling the lie that life is something we achieve. And people are believing it.

On the surface, helping people to become their ideal selves and work to achieve the ideal society seems noble. But at what cost? I know we all long to return to Eden or finally reach "the city to come," but all this spiritual blood, sweat, and tears is keeping us from the real question: What would you do if you knew you were already held by a love that will never let you go?

What we're really asking is: What are we trusting? There is joy when we finally realize that trust in Jesus alone is our greatest need. The question for us in Reclaim 3 is: What does that trust accomplish in our lives, and why does it matter so much?

JESUS, FRIEND OF SINNERS

Speaking of Eden, it all went to pot there, didn't it? Theologians call it "the fall" for a reason. Since the first act of disobedience in the garden, mankind has been dead in its unbelief (Rom. 3:23). While some argue this forbidden fruit scene is just religious folklore, it's kind of hard to look around, even honestly look at ourselves, and deny that something is seriously broken.

Some people deny the existence of sin and deem everything relative. However, no matter where you go in the world, you'll find a society that has a list of beliefs or behaviors that are acceptable and not acceptable. Even here in America, a country that prides itself on being "tolerant," we find extreme intolerance of specific, well, sins.

Where we differ is in our solution to sin.

For many, the answer to the problem of sin is to get people to sin less, which is why we've created rehabilitation programs, classes on ethics, discipleship programs, a ten billion dollar a year self-help industry, and a "cancel culture." Politics and policies, education and entertainment, movements for more freedom and more restraint—they have all tried to heal our sense of brokenness. But in the end, all these inventions have fallen short. They cannot, and will never, change the heart of man.

Of course, the Scriptures acknowledge the truth about the human condition. In Ephesians 2:1, the Apostle Paul described the state of humanity as those who are "dead in... trespasses and sins." He also viewed himself as someone beyond repair and in need of rescue (Rom. 7:24-25).

God's response to humanity's collective fall was the sinless "fall" of God himself in Christ. Jesus descended from the Father's right hand to die on a cross in our stead. He went down into the grave only to be raised in our stead, for our justification (Rom. 3:24).

There is no greater expression of love, Jesus said, than to lay down one's life for one's friends (Jn. 15:13). As a friend of sinners, Jesus did just that (Jn. 11:25).

THE GOD WHO LOST COUNT

Continuing our conversation from Reclaim 1 about reconciliation in Colossians 1:20, Paul gets even more specific in 2 Corinthians 5:18-19 when he says, "All this is from God, who through Christ *reconciled* us to himself and gave us the ministry of reconciliation; that is, in Christ *God was reconciling the world to himself, not counting their trespasses against them...*" (emphasis ours).

Here, Paul doubles down on this cosmic reconciled reality in Christ and goes a bit further. He says that God, for the sake of Jesus, is not counting their trespasses (sins) against "them" (the world).

Well, Paul, how can that be?

2 Corinthians 5:21 says, "For our sake he made him to be sin who knew no sin, so that in him we might become the righteousness of God."

We don't have a problem saying, "Jesus died for our sins," but the language in the Scriptures is a bit more forceful and provocative. Did Jesus really take upon himself the sin of the whole world? The answer: Yes. In the cross, God reckons your sin as belonging to Jesus (imputation). Jesus was "made...to be sin." Sin was imputed to Jesus and he died to make satisfaction for the sins of the world. That is an objective fact.

Sin has already been paid for in the dying and rising of Jesus. God's heart toward the world is already forgiving. With Scripture as our highest authority, we can boldly say that the world is already forgiven. The religious scorekeeping has ended. God lost count.

AWAKENING TO THIS REALITY

The salvation that Christ accomplished and brought to the world can only be described as a gift. Ephesians 2:8 says, "For by grace you have been saved through faith. And this is not your own doing; it is the gift of God, not a result of works, so that no one may boast."

What then does one do upon hearing that the whole job is already done in Christ? Since work has ceased and salvation is a gift, a response is the only thing left. The only appropriate response is trust and elation.

We're trying to help you see a very subtle, but life-giving truth—faith isn't the final piece of an almost finished puzzle or the final infinity stone in the infinity gauntlet (allowing it to finally be effective); rather, it is something that simply enables us to relate to someone else who has already done whatever needs doing. Faith, therefore, is not what's needed for us to "get in"; rather, it's the discovery of what already is. When someone, by God's grace, awakens to the reconciling and justifying King known as Jesus, they awaken to a reality that is already fixed, sealed, and finished.

AN ANALOGY FROM NEVERLAND

In the movie *Hook*, Peter Pan (now a middle-aged, successful but unimaginative workaholic lawyer named Peter Banning) sits down with the Lost Boys at a table for dinner. A marvelous feast sits in front of them, ready to be devoured, but there's just one problem: Peter can't see the food set before him because of his lack of imagination (read "faith). Already "hangry," Pan grows more and more frustrated as he watches others enjoy their food while he stares at an empty table. Up to this point, he has resisted using his imagination because he views the mentality of the Lost Boys and the way of life in Neverland as childish and reckless. This dinner scene is yet another instance where the maturity of his current life clashes with the foolishness of his former life.

After being baited into an insult match with Rufio, Peter's imagination and childishness kick in as he begins to exchange insults with the one who had become the leader of the Lost Boys in his absence. Eventually, Pan wins. Rufio is silenced. In a final blow to Rufio's reign, Pan dips a spoon into a pot of rainbow-colored mashed potatoes (which he cannot see). Cocking it back, Pan tells Rufio to "go suck on a dead dog's nose," then flings the food in Rufio's face. Immediately, Pan's eyes are opened. He can now enjoy the feast that has been right under his nose the entire time.

Faith relates to the finished work of Jesus in a very similar way. Our good and gracious Host has prepared a table for the world. Everything needed to dine in fellowship with him has been taken care of by the Host himself. We are already invited and included as beloved guests. We need only open our eyes.

THE UNEASINESS OF GRACE

This kind of indiscriminate inclusion usually creates a bit of awkward tension, especially among those who have been awake at Jesus' table for a while. The truth is, we live in a world obsessed with progress, performance, and the myth of control. The idea of God justifying sinners solely on the life, death, and resurrection of his Son, the idea of attributing his righteousness to broken people through faith alone, seems crazy. We are prone to the belief that it takes more than just faith alone to become a disciple of Jesus. Studying the parables of Jesus reveals this proclivity.

For instance, have you ever noticed the badness of the parables' good characters? To make sure his point is about our need for faith and not good works, the only characters Jesus rewards in the parables are the un-reformed. The younger brother who gets the welcome home party is as wild and self-centered as they come, and his older brother, who's upset and won't come to the party, is a guy who has always done what is right. The laborers who get paid a full day's wage for only an hour of work are freeloaders, while the all-day laborers who get pushed to the end of the line are the "responsible" employees. The wise virgins, the bridesmaids, who ignore the needs of others with their noses in the air enjoy the party with the bridegroom, while the bridesmaids who left out of a desire to better themselves come back to find they are not welcomed. The list goes on with the same theme: salvation isn't about behaving better. It's about faith in the work of God on our behalf!

As humans, we resort to motive-correcting and behavior-adjusting as a means of obtaining and/or maintaining salvation. Since this is our default, it's wise to test our hearts. What are we believing?

TWO MEN WALK INTO A TEMPLE

Look at the parable Jesus told about the Pharisee and the tax collector in Luke 18:9-14. The tax collector is a Jewish man working as a thief for their oppressor, the Roman government. To help you grasp this, imagine ISIS taking over the US. One of your friends goes to work for them. He aims to help them obtain the financial support they need to stay in power, and he does so by taking the money from your pocket. Since your friend is in a position of power, he begins to treat you, your spouse, and your children in any way he pleases. He'd be considered a traitor to his fellow countrymen. In the same way, a Jew becoming a tax collector meant he was a traitor to his people. He exploited them.

Jesus says the tax collector stands in the Temple with his head bowed; he admits that he's not only a loser, but he's as good as dead, with absolutely nothing to offer. Jesus then says this man went home "justified." The Pharisee, on the other hand, has spent his life pursuing righteousness in obedience to the law of God. This is beyond anything you have ever seen. He lays out a list of all his good deeds. "Hey, God, here's a report card on all the sins from which I have been abstaining, along with a list of all the good works I have been carrying out." He then proceeds to thank God he's "not like this other man," this tax collector. He's a self-proclaimed winner, and Jesus says he goes home just as he came in—dead in his sins.

We hear this story and, if we're honest, we're often appalled at the arrogance of the Pharisee, all the while knowing we are just as broken, flawed, and foolish as the tax collector. Yet, while we praise God for his love and grace, we still hesitate to extend that same grace to others.

A PERSONAL STORY

This was my (Russ') story for years until one day when I read Between Noon and Three by Robert Capon. Based on everything I'd heard about the book, I was hesitant to read it. The idea of being saved by grace alone through faith alone in Jesus alone was something I held to, but was adamant about one's faith resulting in right behavior. I considered myself a "gospel guy" but was suspicious of those who over-emphasized grace—fearing it would lead to spiritual laziness or a lack of fruit in the church I was leading. To find the ammunition I needed to disprove Capon's claims, I opted to pick up a copy of his book.

I eventually came across his take on the parable mentioned above (Lk. 18:9-14), and I'd be lying if I told you I didn't desire to catch him transgressing in his interpretation of the text. As I began considering the questions Capon posed, it occurred to me that I had never considered what Jesus declared in this parable through the lens of what the tax collector would do next.

The following are a series of questions that Capon led me to consider.

Follow the tax collector home in your mind's eye and as he goes through the ensuing week. What do you want to see him doing in those coming days? I naturally made a list: stop stealing, stop lying, give back the money he took, quit his job, etc.

Now, imagine the tax collector goes back to the Temple one week later with nothing in his life reformed, and God again declares him justified as he admits his death. Do you like that? "Hell no!" I said. In fact, the thought made me throw the book down. "This is the kind of thinking that leads to lawlessness!" But curiosity soon won and, with it, the following question: Now, take the tax collector back to the Temple the following week with some reform under his belt: less lying, less stealing, etc. Do you want God to talk with him about the extent to which he mended his ways this past week? Of course, I did. And as I read on, that's when it hit me between the eyes: Why am I, and almost every believer I know, so hell-bent on destroying the story Jesus is telling?

Why do we desire to send the tax collector back to the Temple with the Pharisee's report card in his pocket and his speech in hand? If this parable teaches us anything, it's that Jesus isn't interested in speeches and lists.

The belief that our spiritual resumés count for anything keeps us from the one thing that does: the admission of our death and exclusive trust in the One who grants mercy and gives grace. According to Jesus, that act of faith alone awakens us to him and the table he's prepared. As I dwelt on this fact, my heart swelled with joy over God's grace, but I began to think through my usual pushbacks.

And there were plenty.

PUSHBACK #1
If it's a work of grace, then why does the Bible talk about our repentance?

Contrary to what I learned from sermons and in school, the word "repent" is an invitation to change your mind, not a bitter ultimatum to start living right. The translation of the Greek word metanoia means "turn your mind around," not "change your behavior."

Phrases like Jesus' call to "repent and believe" in Mark 1:15 have often been referenced to imply a two-step process of true saving faith, but this shouldn't be read as two separate acts. It's not, "Repent first, and once you've done that, then believe." Instead, the words Jesus used are a double imperative doing duty for a conditional statement of a single truth.

For example, the proverb, "Spare the rod and spoil the child," means, "If you spare the rod, you will automatically spoil the child." The two are different sides of the same coin. To "repent and believe" means that when you turn to Jesus as your only hope, you are, at that moment, believing. In other words, repenting and believing happen together as one act of faith.

Another passage I thought of in my fear of people abusing grace was the call to have "works worthy of repentance" in Acts 26:20. This phrase is used by Paul, who was once a great persecutor of the Church, as he explains his conversion story to Agrippa.

Since Paul was declaring the death and resurrection of Jesus alone as his (and our) only hope, the phrase "works worthy of repentance" can only mean having fruit in our lives from Jesus, which declares our belief in him rather than our unbelief. We believe that fruit results from faith. We just believe that fruit comes because of the promise and work of Jesus in and through us, rather than through our own pursuit. More on that in Reclaim 4.

Remember, the gospel is actual good news, not potential good news. It's an announcement that something has already taken place, not a proposition. Brennan Manning, in his book *The Ragamuffin Gospel,* clarifies how repentance relates to salvation: "The gospel of grace announces: Forgiveness precedes repentance. The sinner is accepted before he pleads for mercy. It is already granted. He need only receive it. Total amnesty. Gratuitous pardon." [1]

---

[1] Brennan Manning, The Ragamuffin Gospel: Good News for the Bedraggled, Beat-Up, and Burnt Out (Sisters, Oregon, Multnomah, 2000), page 181.

PUSHBACK #2
If becoming and living as a disciple of Jesus is an act of faith alone, then what do we do with the call to "works" (as seen in James)?

James 2:17 says, "... faith by itself, if it does not have works, is dead." In John 14:21, Jesus basically says, "Those who love Me obey Me, and so prove to be My disciples." These were the hallmark verses I used when confronting my life or the lives of those who were walking in a way contrary to Jesus. However, in light of what Jesus declared on the cross and over and over throughout the parables, it dawned on me that these passages are promises, not marching orders.

Every passage must be read in its immediate context and must be interpreted in view of all that Jesus has done and declared (broad gospel context). Without the declaration of, "It is finished," as a broad interpretive lens, you can mistake James' words as a call to prove your faith is real by doing and maintaining a certain amount of works. Instead, James is pointing out what we've always known about works: they're intended for our neighbors, as in, people we actually know. Faith, by itself, can't help the sister who is poorly clothed and lacking daily food in James 2. Saying to someone in need, "I hope you find food and shelter soon," while offering no practical help is akin to "thoughts and prayers." It's a heartfelt sentiment when you live far away from a difficult situation with limited ability to tangibly help, but a heartless act when someone cold and hungry is standing at your door.

PUSHBACK #3
If simple faith is all that is required, what should we make of passages like Luke 14:25-27? Jesus seems to be talking about the cost of becoming a disciple.

"If anyone comes to me and does not hate his own father and mother and wife and children and brothers and sisters, yes, and even his own life, he cannot be my disciple."

Jesus' words here in Luke 14:26 seem harsh and contradictory to his call to faith alone, until you understand that family was of utmost importance to his Jewish audience. They trusted and relied upon their lineage, their inheritance, and the legacy they would leave above everything else. It was a point of righteousness, legacy they would leave above everything else. It was a point of righteousness, their sense of "enoughness." This long list of family members that Jesus points to represents the constructs and identities we've established for ourselves outside of the One who made us. The call to discipleship here is nothing more or less than a call to believe in Jesus alone—to attach our faith and trust to the better object in Jesus. To die to the idea that Instagram "likes," paychecks, sexuality, political views, parenting skills, curated kitchens, food choices, and religious or social performance could ever be enough is the invitation here. Jesus said that the "will of God" in our lives is to "believe in the Son" (John 6:29).

This invitation to hate the competing cultural identities that rob you of what you need and long for in Jesus alone is followed by two examples of trying to accomplish something without enough resources:

- Building a tower without sufficient resources (Lk.14:28-30)
- Battling a king who has twenty thousand men when you only have ten thousand (Lk.14:31-32)

It's another way of saying, "Do the math." You're already in a losing position. The law of God demands perfect righteousness on your part and it's not looking good. Recognize your current state. Admit your death. Confess your inability. Which leads us to Luke 14:27 and the call to "bear your own cross."

Since the cross is no longer the chosen method of execution used in our day, it's easy to mistake Jesus' command to, "Take up your cross and follow me," as some radical call to discipleship rather than a call to faith. So, exchange the word "cross" for a modern form of capital punishment like lethal injection. This helps us better grasp what Jesus is saying here.

This is not a call to ascend the hill of Christianity with a cross on our back, but an invitation to descend the hill of spiritual aspiration into our grave. "Ambitious" is no way to describe someone who's just received a lethal injection. This is a shockingly vivid way to drive home the importance of embracing our death (or total inability/insufficiency) as the means to life with God. The good news is that "take up your cross" isn't a call to level-up in your faith or an impossible challenge for only the most sincerely spiritual; instead, it's a recognition of our inability to do so. To follow Jesus, one simply needs to lose the illusion of life apart from him who is "life" so they can cling to the only One who is in the resurrection business.

In other words, admit that you're the tax collector, and die to the idea that somehow you have a list of your own earthly accomplishments or identities that are worth anything in comparison to Jesus. Sadly, these passages have often been occasions to push the broken and struggling away from Jesus rather than propel us towards him.

This lopsided view of God and how we relate to him (or how we become disciples) might frustrate you, but that doesn't make it any less true. This one-sided telling of the Good News is the essence of grace, something we've mentioned in Reclaim 1 and Reclaim 2, but have yet to define.

ONE-WAY LOVE

In our opinion, the best definition of grace comes from Paul Zahl's book *Grace In Practice*:

> Grace is love that seeks you out when you have nothing to give in return. Grace is love coming at you that has nothing to do with you. Grace is being loved when you are unlovable … . The cliché definition of grace is "unconditional love." It is a true cliché, for it is a good description of the thing. Let's go a little further, though. Grace is a love that has nothing to do with you, the beloved. It has everything and only to do with the lover. Grace is irrational in the sense that it has nothing to do with weights and measures. It has nothing to do with my intrinsic qualities or so-called "gifts" (whatever they may be). It reflects a decision on the part of the giver, the one who loves, in relation to the receiver, the one who is loved, that negates any qualifications the receiver may personally hold … Grace is one-way love.

Sure, this message of reckless grace and scandalous love clashes with our law-loving, fix-it-yourself hearts. However, if there were anything more for us to do, anything we had to bring to the table, we would never make it to dinner.

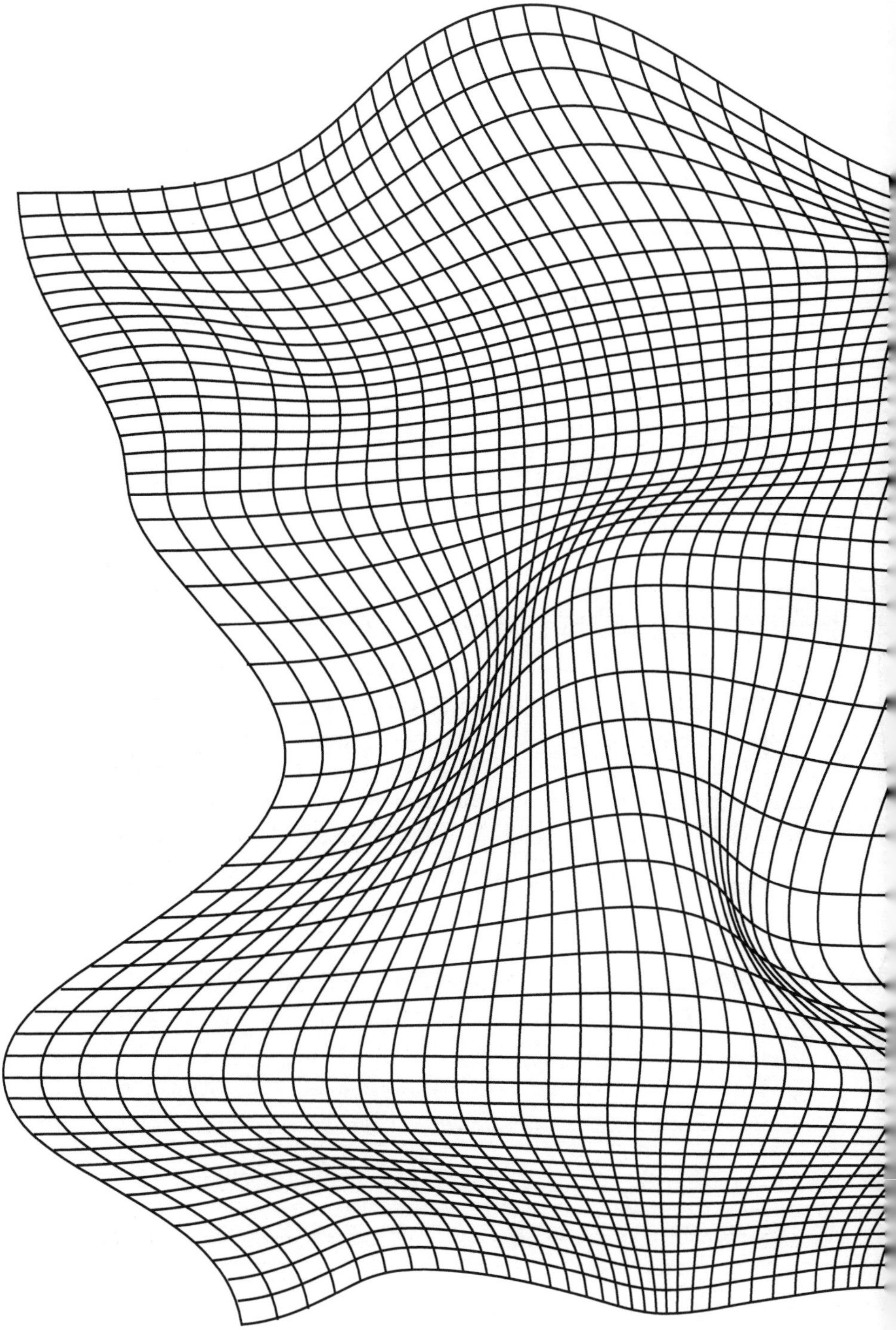

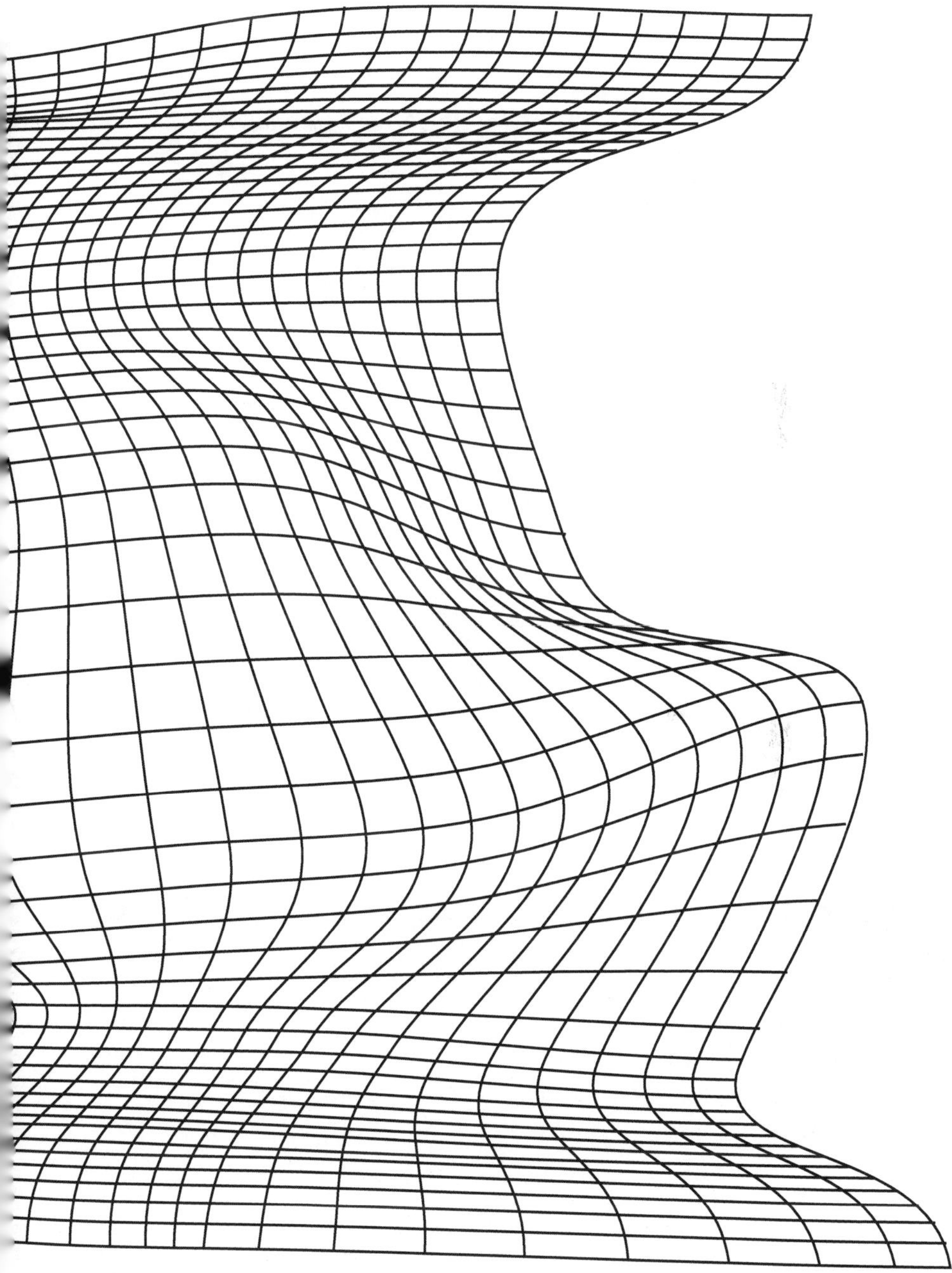

4

RECLAIM 4

REST

In his book *The Prodigal God*, Tim Keller explains that it isn't correct to refer to the parable Jesus told in Luke 15 as "The Prodigal Son" because it begins with Jesus saying, "There was a man who had two sons" (Lk. 15:11). The whoremongering younger brother who wished his father dead took his inheritance and spent it all on partying with prostitutes. Even after hitting rock bottom, he continued his selfish lifestyle as he made his way back home; at least there he could be one of his father's hired hands. In contrast—at least on the surface—the older brother was quite the opposite. This hard-working, self-centered control freak was always one you could depend on, not because of his genuine love for God and others, but because he was pursuing the accolades he could pile up through his prideful performance.

Two brothers, both equally dead. One dying in his rebellion, the other in his self-righteousness. This is neither a story about the irresponsible younger brother, nor the responsible older one. Instead, it's a story about a prodigal father who pursues both sons with reckless love.

As people who, like the younger and older brothers, are all equally dying in one of two camps, we rejoice in a God who has recklessly pursued us all. We rejoice that salvation is something made possible by Jesus alone and received by faith alone as a gift from God (Eph. 2:8-9). Yet something in us often moves our focus away from a life full of grace in God and towards a life of performance. So we need to be reminded that the grammar of Christianity is replacement, not improvement.

REPLACEMENT THEOLOGY

For us, replacement theology refers not to an eschatological idea but to the need for broken people (the only kind of people there are) to look outside of themselves for redemption. We need rescue. Jesus knew he would replace our broken, foolish, flawed lives with his perfect, faithful, obedient life. That's why his mission, one even his disciples didn't fully grasp while they were with him, was to die. Jesus knew it would be his work of living a perfect life under the law, dying the death sinners deserved, and rising victoriously from the dead that ultimately mattered. He knew our lives would be hidden completely in him (Col. 3). He knew that we would be set "free" from the law of sin and death (Rom. 8:2; Gal. 5:1).

Here are some verses to consider when thinking about the reality of replacement:

Galatians 2:20 says that we "have been crucified with Christ. It is no longer [we] who live, but Christ who lives in [us]." You and I no longer live, Paul says.

Colossians 3:1-4 says, "If then you have been raised with Christ, seek the things that are above, where Christ is, seated at the right hand of God. Set your minds on things that are above, not on things that are on earth. For you have died, and your life is hidden with Christ in God. When Christ who is your life appears, then you also will appear with him in glory." Like a tiny bookmark lost inside a gigantic novel or rebar hidden within a wall of concrete, we are hidden in Christ. We are forever united to Jesus (who he is, what he's done, and what he will do). Far from insignificant, our jumbled lives have sunk deeply and securely into the resurrected Christ.

Romans 8:1 says, "There is therefore now no condemnation for those who are in Christ Jesus." There is no independent "you" to condemn when you're crucified and hidden in the righteous One.

Hebrews 10:10 says, "... we have been sanctified through the offering of the body of Jesus Christ once for all." Verse 14 of the same chapter says that this once for all sacrifice has "perfected [us] for all time." We are now perfect in Jesus. It's not on us to become like God because our sin was placed on the second Adam, who achieved what the first Adam could not (Rom. 5:12-21). Turns out God is not a

God of second chances. It's much more hopeful than that. As Tullian Tchividjian pointed out, "[God] is a God of one chance and a second Adam." [1]

Knowing he would literally be our substitute and stand in our place, Jesus was able to slow down, meet people where they were, speak to the root of life, and offer rest. "Come to me all who labor and are heavy laden, and I will give you rest." This is the invitation Jesus offers our exhausted world (Matt. 11:28-30). Even today, he addresses the longings of our heart, while simultaneously making it feel like it's going to jump out of our chest. This is the deep inhale and long exhale that comes from knowing "it is finished" and I am loved (Jn. 19:28-30).

IMPROVEMENT THEOLOGY

Part of the human condition is an infatuation with progress and performance. People believe the problems in their lives stem from inactivity, so they're invigorated by charging ahead and doing more. It's a theology of improvement.

Sure, we believe Jesus brought us into the Kingdom through his death and resurrection, and we believe it is by faith alone that we awaken to this new life. Yet, many of us also believe we must now get our act together and bear fruit as evidence of our salvation. We read passages about being "doers of the Word" as if these passages are an island to themselves, independent of all that Jesus claimed, independent of the fact that we "no longer live" (James 2; Gal. 2).

It's a paradigm we see played out all the time. Our faith, which is to be in a Person who is "unseen," is instead sadly placed in what we can "see." Our faith becomes about our progress or lack thereof (2 Cor. 4:18).

Sadly, this kind of approach to Christianity makes the Christian life the focus instead of Christ Himself. The result? Either pride in your discipline and accomplishments, or burn out and shame in your failures.

WHAT FRUIT-BEARING IS AND ISN'T

Christ is our Creator, and by faith in his death for us, the flawed, independent self that has been crucified and replaced with the perfect Son becomes our life, our reality. Contrary to popular belief, we didn't need a guide. We needed a

---

1 Tullian Tchividjian, https://www.tullian.net/articles/i-failed-to-become-like-daddy-bill

Savior. A guide says, "Go that way." A Savior says, "You can't, but I did it for you."

Understanding this opens our eyes to what we saw in John 19, where Jesus announced that his Father's dealings with the sins of this world are "finished." This is far different than the idea that his work is "to be continued." The sins we personally struggle with, as well as the ones committed against us, have already been bested in Christ. In the risen Christ we stand!

Let's consider a few questions in light of what we've read:

How then should we view fruit and progress in the Christian life?

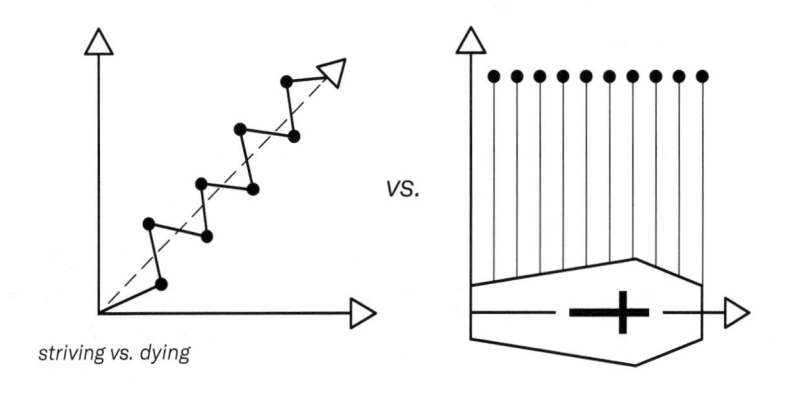

striving vs. dying

Above are two diagrams that illustrate growth in righteousness over the timeline of our lives. One imagines spiritual progress through the lenses of improvement theology (left), and the other through the lens of replacement theology (right).

On the left, we illustrate the belief that God is at work to improve our behavior and character. The line angling upwards represents the journey to bear fruit through obedience in both the mountain top experiences and the dreary days in the valley. You begin by faith, receive help from the Holy Spirit in the form of something like a jet-pack, and over time become more righteous as you bear "better" fruit. This popular illustration is deceiving for a number of reasons, but the main one is that it reinforces the heart's natural modus operandi that somehow we are still alive in our own efforts to climb the ladder of progress. This is the opposite of "take up your cross."

On the right, we illustrate that God's plan for our flesh wasn't to improve it but to kill it and replace it with his perfect Son. We were "...crucified with Christ" (Gal. 2:20). As we recognize our death and daily cling to Jesus as our only hope, the Spirit bears perfect fruit through our walking "corpse." It comes from daily dying to the project of self, not striving. In fact, our efforts to wrangle the flesh into submission are not only useless, they're sinful because all too often control and independence are found at the core of our striving.

Two key statements to consider from the book of Galatians:

- Galatians 5:6: "For in Christ Jesus neither circumcision [rule keeping] nor uncircumcision [rule breaking] counts for anything, but only faith [dead to our performance and looking outside of ourselves to Jesus] working through love."

- Galatians 6:15: "For neither circumcision [religion] counts for anything, nor uncircumcision [irreligion], but a new creation [root]."

Paul is teaching us the same thing Jesus taught in the parable of the two lost sons, where Jesus confronted the common understanding of his day that you were either a lawbreaker or a law keeper. The scriptures are clear that law breaking and law keeping, inactivity and activity, circumcision and uncircumcision are all worth nothing (Gal. 5:6). Fleshly righteousness is a worthless counterfeit for the perfect righteousness of God that is born in us by the Spirit of Christ!

His righteousness is perfect because it is neither ours, nor of us. God fulfills his commands in us by way of his Son. This is a change that is not of us, one that our friends will generally recognize in our lives before we will. In other words, the fruit of the Spirit (law-keeping, obedience) isn't something we aim at in advance, but something we notice in hindsight. This is why Paul in Galatians 5:23 says of bearing fruit in the Spirit, "... there is no law" that can produce this.

Doesn't the use of spiritual disciplines help us progress in our obedience to God?

"We're all messed up, but we're working on it" is a statement often heard in the Church. People tend to see God as the One who gave "spiritual disciplines" (think rhythms of church attendance, Scripture reading, prayer, fasting, and solitude) in order to help grow them in their obedience to Jesus. Oftentimes, the thought process is, "The more we do, the better we get, and the more God moves on our behalf." Although this idea is popular and these practices are good, they aren't "disciplines" God has told us to aim at in order to progress in the Christian life. Instead, they are things we walk in as the Spirit leads. In short, Scripture reading, prayer, fasting, and solitude aren't a list to keep. We walk in them when God leads us in them (Eph. 2:10, Phil. 2:13).

There's something in us that always wants to shift away from Jesus as the perfect connection point with God. We lean toward our performance and the things we believe we should do to connect with God or get him to move in our lives, which leads to the opposite of rest. So for all our performance-trusting hearts, let's remember that according to Scripture, God despises our attempts to improve ourselves in the hopes of making ourselves righteous. To do so is to announce our unbelief in the One who has already made us righteous (2 Cor. 5:21; Gal. 2:21, 5:1-4).

By no means does this prevent the declaration of what is good and joyful to walk in. It doesn't mean we should neglect scripture, prayer, community, fasting, and wrestling with temptation. It just changes the posture of our pursuit. Everything we do from here on out is done from a place of Spirit-led desire under the banner: IT IS FINISHED!

But if this is true, why am I still struggling with sin?

Assuring people that Jesus saves by faith alone tends to raise eyebrows and questions. You can tell that the Apostle Paul's message of grace was also met with some common questions regarding behavior. On one occasion, he addressed the concern that grace would surely give people an excuse to live rebelliously and selfishly. "Are we to continue in sin so that grace may abound?" Paul asked. "By no means! How can we who died to sin still live in it?" (Rom 6:1-2).

It's easy to read the word "sin" in verse 1 as a verb (the act of sinning) and wonder, when honest with ourselves about the areas we still struggle in, if we are authentic Christians. However, Paul actually uses the word te hamartia, which is not a verb at all. Instead, it's a noun referring to our identity! To go on in the state of "sin" is impossible for someone who is "in Christ" because the old Adam (our old lives) has been replaced by the new Adam (Jesus, who is our life).

Paul continues to drive home this reality of our death and the myth of an independent "you" (by way of union with Jesus in his death):

- We were baptized into His death. [v.3]
- We were buried with Jesus. [v.4]
- We have been united with Jesus in His death. [v.5]
- Our old self was crucified. [v.6]
- We died with Christ. [v.8]

Paul is trying to tell us that we died with Christ! He doesn't say, "Sin is dead to us," or, "You should die to sin," or, "Congratulations! You've decided to die to sin! Now what?" Sin is very much alive in our world and in us, but, according to Scripture, these things have been disarmed. Our relationship to sin is forever changed; our reality has undergone a fundamental shift in Jesus Christ. Martin Luther described this reality as simul justus et peccator, meaning that, on this side of life, we are simultaneously just (righteous in Christ) and sinful. One refers to our unchanging identity, the other to our temporary struggle.

Paul is telling us in Romans 6 that we don't need to worry (in an ultimate sense) about sin because Jesus already bested it in his death and resurrection, and he brought us along with him in his victory by faith.

Gerhard Forde describes this reality so well:

> Just the sheer and unconditional announcement "You have died!"—The uncompromising insistence that there is nothing to do now, that God has made his last 'move'—just that, and that alone, is what puts the old being to death, precisely because there is nothing for the old being to do... There is no way for the old being to do anything about this grace. The unconditional justification, the grace itself, slays the old self and destroys its' body of sin' to fashion a new one. It is all over! Christ being raised from the dead will never die again. One can't go back and repeat it. He died to sin once for all, and now He lives to God. Conclusion? You can now only consider yourself dead to sin and alive to God in Christ Jesus! [2]

---

2 Gerhard Forde, Christian Spirituality: Five Views of Sanctification (Downers Grove, IL, IVP, 1988).

What about those who aren't bearing fruit? Or those who are, but still lack so much?

We have a friend who, on the advice of a horticulturalist, planted a peach tree at his house in Chicago. After the first year, he and his wife had some delicious peaches to enjoy. The following year, there was a harsh winter and the tree didn't produce any fruit. With a dead tree in the yard, he invited his horticulture friend over to take a look.

After some tests, she assured him that even though the tree looked dead, it was actually alive. "The tree will bear fruit again," she said. He now had three options. The first option was to disbelieve the professional and chop the tree down. A second option would be to buy peaches from the store and tape them to the tree. Or lastly, he could trust the words of one who knew more than him that one day this tree, that was actually alive, would bear fruit again.

In Jesus, we're free to trust and stop buying tape. Philippians 1:6 says, "... he who began a good work in you will bring it to completion." This is a promise that has nothing to do with our ability to see the fruit or our ability to taste it. For, as 2 Corinthians 4:18 reminds us, our faith focuses "... not on the things that are seen [our progress] but on the things that are unseen [Jesus' work in our lives]."

PROMISES VS. MARCHING ORDERS

This Midwestern peach tree actually reminds us of another passage that deals with the issue of fruit. John 15 has been a popular passage for many in regards to the topic of fruit, sanctification, spiritual progress, etc. Let's take a deeper look at what Jesus is telling us.

> I am the true vine, and my Father is the Vinedresser. Every branch in me that does not bear fruit he takes away, and every branch that does bear fruit he prunes, that it may bear more fruit. Already you are clean because of the word that I have spoken to you. Abide in me, and I in you. As the branch cannot bear fruit by itself, unless it abides in the vine, neither can you, unless you abide in me. I am the vine; you are the branches. Whoever abides in me and I in him, he it is that bears much fruit, for apart from me you can do nothing. If anyone does not abide in me he is thrown away like a branch and withers; and the branches are gathered, thrown into the fire, and burned. If you abide in me, and my words abide in you, ask whatever you wish, and it

will be done for you. By this my Father is glorified, that you bear much fruit and so prove to be my disciples. As the Father has loved me, so have I loved you. Abide in my love. If you keep my commandments, you will abide in my love, just as I have kept my Father's commandments and abide in his love. These things I have spoken to you, that my joy may be in you, and that your joy may be full." (John 15:1-11)

Some introductory points should be made:

1. Notice that you and I are called "branches." In our experience, most believers approach their spiritual progress as if they are in charge of their own spiritual health and growth; but branches don't produce fruit— they "bear" fruit.

2. This point is connected to the first. You and I are not the "Vinedresser"—the Father is. In fact, since Jesus is the "vine," we're not even the tree. Instead, we're the "branches" that do "nothing" except abide in the "vine." In a very real way, we are not in control of what is happening in this field.

With these simple observations in place, let's take a look at the text. In verse 2a, Jesus says, "Every branch in me that does not bear fruit he takes away..." Hmmm... what to do with a branch that doesn't bear fruit? This is the worst case scenario for most church leaders who think they need to present their churches as spotless someday; and it is a fearful consideration for most Christians who have been told their whole lives that genuine believers bear fruit and false believers don't. In fact, this passage has been used to "prove" that theory.

A small little thing to point out about this branch before getting to the good news: Jesus tells us this branch is a "branch in [him]." We take this to mean what the phrase "in him" means throughout all of Scripture—this branch is united to the Vine (Jesus).

So what does Jesus do with this fruitless branch? Or a more pointed question: what does God do with us when we don't bear fruit? Jesus says that the Father (the Vinedresser) "takes [it] away." Some have connected the phrase "takes away" to the judgment phrase in verse 6, where some branches are "thrown away."

I (Tony) have taught this in the past, but don't anymore due to one simple detail. The verse 6 branches that are gathered for the burn pile are those who don't "abide."

I know we love to attach all sorts of spiritual disciplines to the word "abide," but the word simply refers to the permanence of our union and relationship with the Vine (by faith). The biggest clue to this is in verse 4 where Jesus says, "Abide in me, and I in you." If abiding strictly refers to early morning prayer and journaling, I have a hard time picturing Jesus abiding in us like that.

But back to the phrase "takes away." The phrase in Greek is *airei*, and it's better translated "to raise, take up, lift," referring to a common practice in Israeli viticulture.

In Jesus' day, grape vines grew on the ground, not suspended in air. In the spring, those caring for these fields would carefully "lift" and "raise" the branches off the ground. The reason for this is that the branches tended to produce hundreds of little tiny roots that would sink into the surface of the soil where there was not sufficient moisture to produce anything but little sour grapes. But if the workers lifted the branches up off the ground, then they would get their moisture from the main vine (and roots) that went deep into the soil.

In some cases, when a branch was struggling to bear fruit, the vine workers would lift it off the ground and better position it with sticks and rocks in order to expose the entire vine to the sun and allow air flow underneath, thus controlling the ripening of the fruit.

In light of this ancient technique, read verse 2 this way: "Every branch in Me that does not bear fruit He raises up." What is the job of the Vinedresser? He goes through the vineyard looking for fruit. But here is a branch on the ground, not bearing any fruit. What does he do? Cut it off? Throw it in the fire? No. He raises it up and cares for it so it will bear fruit! This understanding changes everything.

A few more observations to tie up the loose ends:

    1. Believers, at times, don't bear fruit. Some talk about fruit as if we should

be producing it quickly and constantly, similar to how a factory cranks out widgets. We find comfort in the organic imagery of viticulture.

2. If verse 2 were intended to be a warning against those who don't bear fruit instead of the promise of our faithful Father/Vinedresser to care for us, then verse 11 would have to read, "These things I have spoken to you, that you may be warned (or challenged)." Instead, it reads, "These things I have spoken to you, that my joy may be in you, and that your joy may be full." Joy comes from good news and promises.

3. Jesus follows up verse 2 by saying, "Already you are clean because of the word that I have spoken to you." He's reminding them that they are safe, secure, clean, and holy because he has declared it, not because of the amount of fruit they bear.

4. "By this my Father is glorified, that you bear much fruit and so prove to be my disciples." In light of these things, we can view phrases like this one in verse 8 as promises, not marching orders. Jesus is promising us that because of our union with him (by faith) and the faithful care of our Father/Vinedresser, we WILL bear fruit.

In short, God has invited us to live by faith, to be more convinced by what he's said through the Scriptures than by what we see in our lives or in the lives of those we disciple. We're thankful for the freedom found in his finished work and his promises. It frees us from a radically introspective life that is constantly evaluating and scrutinizing our own progress and the progress of others. Living in light of God's grace and promises allows me to live a life of total dependence. After all, what else can a branch do? "Apart from me you can do nothing."

GRACE IS SUFFICIENT... AND FRUSTRATING

Some call this constant emphasis on God, his promises, and his work in our lives "cheap grace." But grace isn't cheap at all—it's free. We think Steve Brown said it well: "Cheap grace? Listen, if it weren't cheap, you and I couldn't afford it. If it cost us one thing—our commitment, our obedience, our religious actions, or anything else—it would remain in the store on the shelf." [3]

---

3 Steve Brown, A Scandalous Freedom, (Brentwood, Tennesse, Howard Books, 2004).

We understand the frustration of those who cry, "Cheap grace!" They're fearful it will lead to a careless and lawless life (more on that in Reclaim 5). However, the question isn't about whether or not grace is opposed to our efforts, because the point is that grace doesn't need our efforts nor has it ever asked for them. In other words, grace is sufficient. It is enough.

After passionately pleading with God three times for a mysterious "thorn" in his life to be removed, the Apostle Paul was met with a surprising answer (2 Cor. 12:8-9). Instead of God taking this frustrating thing away or even responding with instructions for how to overcome it, God responded by telling him, "My grace is sufficient for you..."

Based on Paul's request, you have to imagine that the answer he received would have been both unexpected and somewhat frustrating. Coming face to face with the "enoughness" of grace is a freeing thing, but it will frustrate you before it frees you. Realizing that grace is sufficient also comes with the discovery that we will never be sufficient.

Death is and always will be a hard pill to swallow, but admitting that and trusting the One whose love is indiscriminate and unending will always lead to rest. Jesus offered that rest not only to Paul in his thorny dilemma but to us all. Matthew 11:28-30 will always be a hallmark verse when it comes to rest, and we like Eugene Peterson's version best. It reads like this:

> Are you tired? Worn out? Burned out on religion? Come to me. Get away with me and you'll recover your life. I'll show you how to take a real rest. Walk with me and work with me — watch how I do it. Learn the unforced rhythms of grace. I won't lay anything heavy or ill-fitting on you. Keep company with me and you'll learn to live freely and lightly.

Grab hold of this good news, friends.

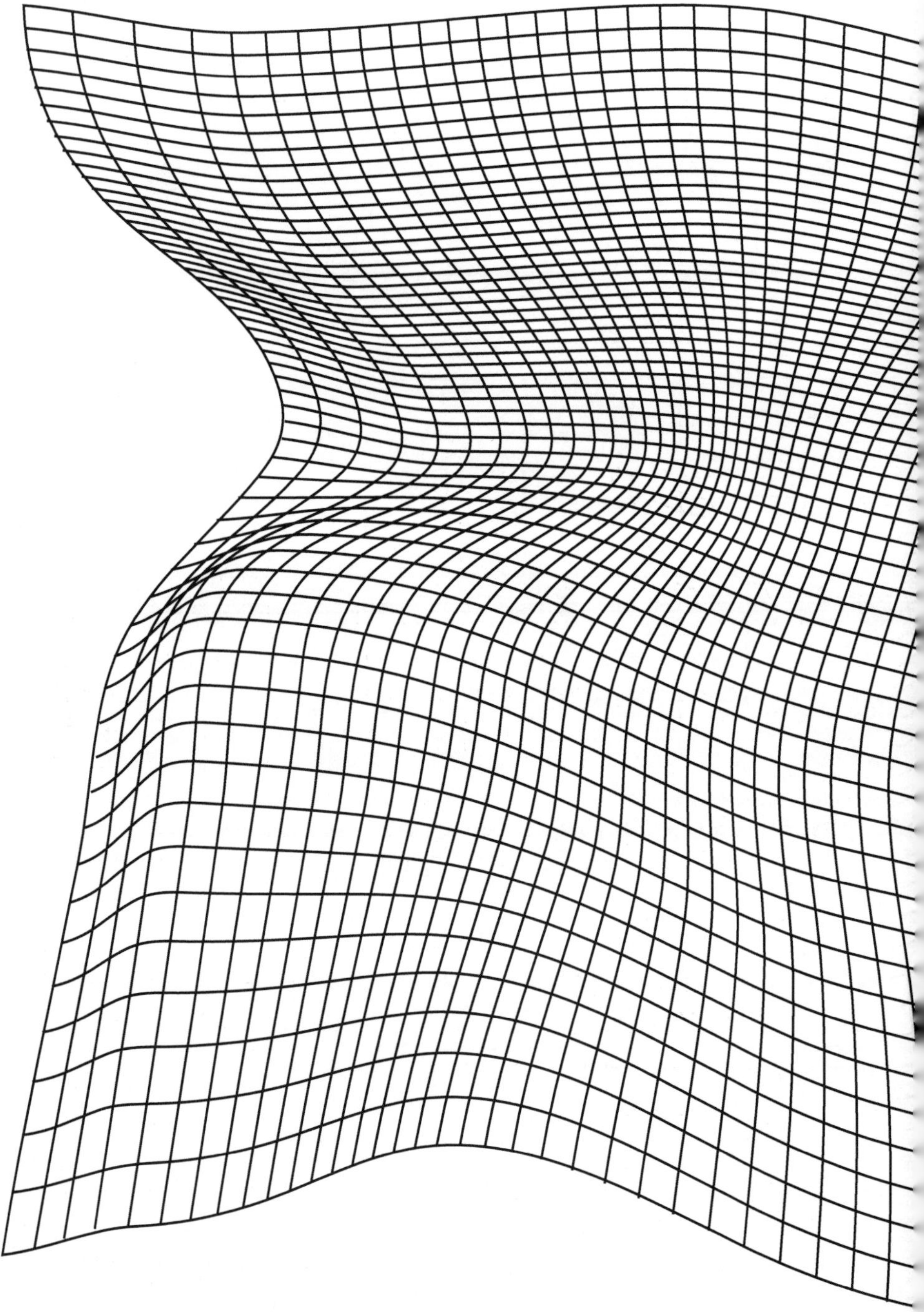

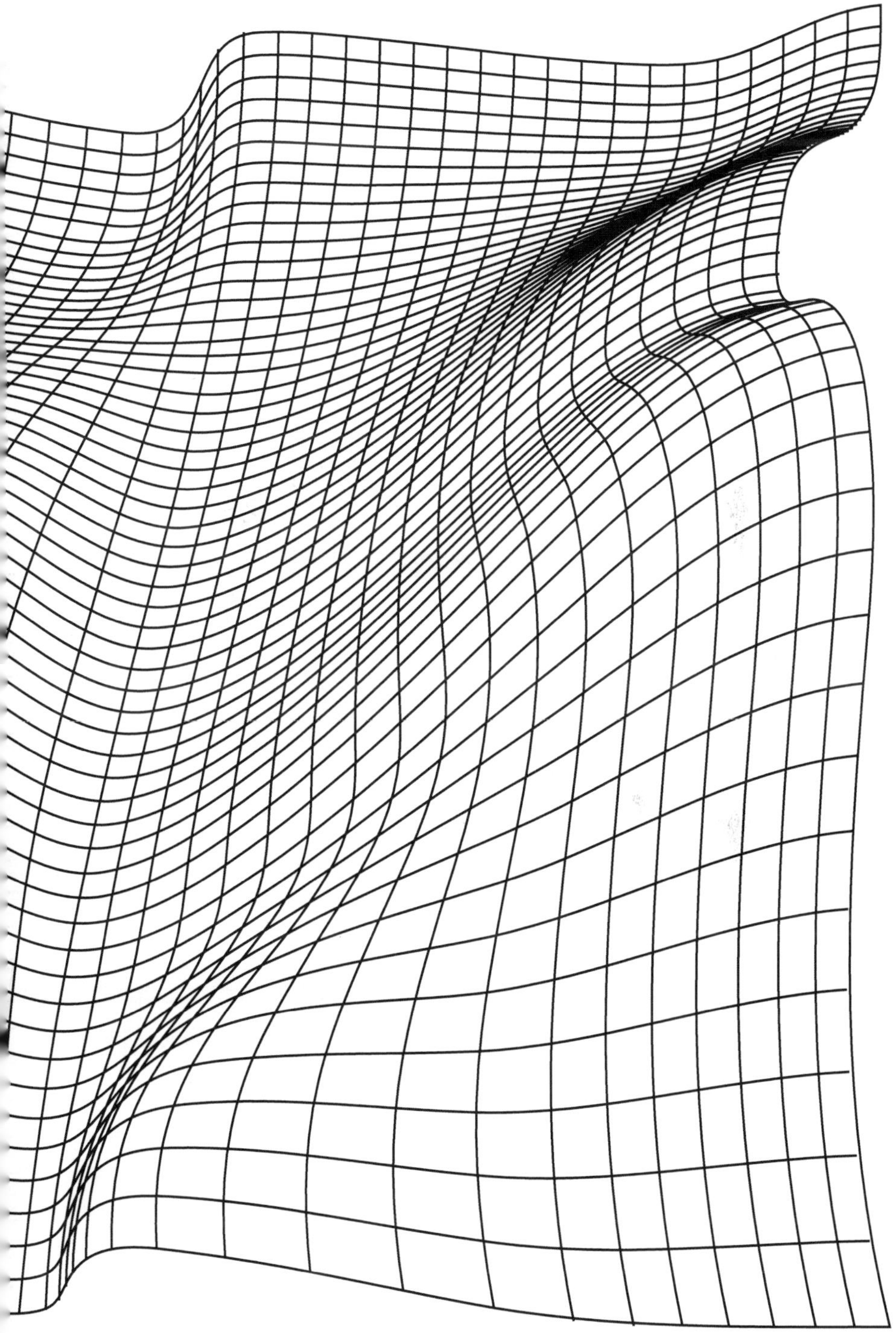

5

RECLAIM 5

WALK

In Reclaim 4, we continued our exploration of God's indiscriminate and incessant love toward sinners—a love that has set us free. The result? Rest. The deep inhale and long exhale that comes from knowing "it is finished" and we are loved.

We now move into a discussion regarding the next question on everyone's mind: how do we walk in this rest? As we seek an answer to this question, we look to the Galatians as a cautionary tale. The Church throughout the region of Galatia had started off strong in the freedom of Jesus (Gal.5:1). They were "running well," Paul said (Gal. 5:7). After beginning a Spirit-empowered life in Jesus, however, they started to think their performance was the key to pleasing God. Because of this, Paul called them "foolish" and told them they had been "bewitched" (tricked) into thinking they needed to now be perfected by the flesh (Gal. 3:1-6).

Dallas Willard famously said, "Grace is not opposed to effort, it is opposed to earning." While we agree that grace and earning are at odds, some nuance is required when it comes to the idea of effort. The Galatian believers understood that salvation wasn't something to be earned, and yet, they caught some passionate criticism from the Apostle Paul for their efforts to sanctify themselves.

While the age-old debate regarding spiritual growth will no doubt continue, we hope to pass on some timeless and timely truths about walking with Jesus.

HARMONY, WITNESS & DEATH

To kick things off, we've found a ton of clarity in considering the wonderful, yet often misunderstood, relationship between law and grace.

The Law of God, as in the moral Law, is a picture of humanity at its finest—thriving in perfect harmony with God and our fellow man. You could call it heaven on earth. But there are a couple of things we must note about the Law:

First, God published the Law and gave it to the Israelites to reveal his perfect character, to instruct them in what was good for them, and to expose the plight of humanity. The Law was not a means to bring them into fellowship; it was a response to the relationship that was already in place by God's doing (Ex. 20:1-3). In other words, the Law followed the relationship, not vice versa.

Second, according to Romans 2:14-16, the Law is inscribed on every human heart, and though it is dulled by our obsession with self-reliance (i.e., sin), our conscience bears witness to what already exists within us. This explains why the moral teachings of non-Christian religions or even secular society are mostly the same as those found in the Bible. The Law is needed—so needed. Jesus himself said that not "...one dot of it shall be removed" (Matt. 5:17).

Third, the Law, which requires 100 percent obedience in thought, word, and deed (Gal. 3:10) was never intended to be the means through which God would rescue sinners and the world sin has marred. Instead, the Law functions as a mirror, showing us our brokenness (Rom. 3:19-20) and our need of God's only plan for rescue—Jesus (Gal. 2:21 + Gal. 3:21-22).

With all this in mind, we can see how the Law brings three necessary and needed things into every nook and cranny of society: (1) harmony, (2) witness, and (3) death. In the Law, we find a picture of what harmony with God and those around us looks like; and by walking in the good things of the Law, we bear witness to the One who brought this harmony into existence. The only issue? We can never walk in the things of the Law on our own. And there, by God's grace, lies the death that leads to life.

TERMS & CONDITIONS APPLY

If you study humanity, you will find that the primary view of God held by people—from past to present—is shaped by a relationship based on conditional promises. We love conditional promises, which is why we keep them at the core of society.

Perform well in school—get into the right college. Go hard in practice—make the team. Excel at work—receive a promotion. Provide all the correct parameters—raise the right kids. This conditional narrative is the same at every turn. However, problems arise when we consider a relationship with God through this same lens. Conditionality forces us to view him as One who always has our file on hand and acts toward us in accordance with how our file reads.

Here, in the practices tied to conditional promises, appears the robbing belief that our relationship is established with God, maintained with God, or lost with God based on how well we hold up our end of the bargain. This explains why we turn the Law, which points to what harmony with God and others looks like, into a ladder we need to climb in order to obtain and maintain our acceptance.

The Good News is that the Kingdom of God doesn't function like a game of Chutes & Ladders. There are no ladders to ascend in a Kingdom where the King descended as a servant to make us "perfect" once and for all (Heb. 10:10-14). Therefore, the "perfect harmony" pictured in the Law is freely available to us in Jesus by grace through faith—never earned.

If we miss this, then the whole point of the Law and grace are buried under the myth that (1) God accepts us if we walk in what he approves of, or (2) God approves of everything we desire because He's already accepted us in his Son. One camp enslaves us to an endless cycle of fear and anxiety, the other, to the pursuit of things that bring hurt in place of the harmony we crave.

The question is: why is this connection so easily missed or ignored?

MAP, MEASURE & MANAGE *(life on our own terms)*

Whether we're talking about religion or the call for a life of morality and justice in the name of "no religion," there seems to be a common thread in the way we approach life. We're talking about humanity's need to be in control.

The popular belief is that we need to use the Law to measure, map, and manage our way to the ideal self and society. We all have an inherent desire to be master of our own destiny, a passion that leaves us feeling either freshly invigorated or fatally incapacitated, depending on how well we perform.

But what if our inherent love affair with progress stands at odds with the actual life God has given us?

Think about it. If Jesus' teachings had followed this narrative, if he had shown up with programs and policies to help us better map, measure, and manage our progress, would the people in power have been furious enough to kill him? Probably not. If Jesus' message were about how he came to improve the improvable, then they would've welcomed him with open arms, and given him a book deal or a new show on Netflix. We love the idea of controlling our own destiny, which is why we cling to experts who claim they can help us do so. We don't crucify them.

Based on how things went for Jesus, we know he was preaching something entirely different than the societal norm. Throughout his journey, he continued to unpack parables about what God was like, all of which were at odds with conditional promises and the desire to measure, map, and manage our way forward. This explains why Jesus continued to say that his mission on earth was to die for and resurrect us, not repair us (Matt. 16; Mk. 10:45).

As One who lived in perfect harmony with the Father and the Spirit, Jesus knew what true harmony is. He knew that not only could we not obtain it on our own, but also that the world would never experience it from his people apart from them living as branches in the Vine (Jn. 15).

Just like Zacchaeus responded to Jesus' love by giving away half of his possessions to the poor and paying back four times the amount he originally extorted (Lk. 19:1-10), so too the fruit that comes from knowing Jesus far exceeds the bare minimum of obeying a law or a rule. Far beyond what we can conjure up by measuring, mapping, and managing our way through life exists the God-given life of "faith, hope, and love."

FAITH, HOPE & LOVE *(the self-forgetful life)*

In Colossians 1:3-6, we find Paul very encouraged by what's happening among the Church in Colossae. In verses 4-5, he mentions their FAITH in Jesus, LOVE for each other, and the HOPE they have in a secure future with God. What's interesting to us is what Paul sites as the source of this fruit. In verse 6,

Paul points to the good news of God's reckless love and indiscriminate grace (gospel) as the cause of this growth, and then, in verse 7, he mentions that their love is finding its source in the Spirit.

The ugly truth about a view of sanctification (spiritual growth) focused on behavior is that it only allows you to grow radically introspective. The cure for humanity's condition has never been found inside ourselves, but rather outside ourselves—in Jesus.

Let's explore the self-forgetful life of faith, hope, and love in a different passage. In 1 Corinthians 13, Paul continues to help the Corinthian believers think through the Christian life. It seems that, in addition to a myriad other things, they'd slipped into some faulty thinking when it came to spiritual growth and maturity—a type of thinking also prevalent today.

In verses 8-12, Paul crushes their (and our) obsession with knowledge and the belief that it equals maturity. Rather than being "mature," he says our obsession with what we can see, know, and understand on this side of eternity is actually "childish." Crazy! What many believers thought made them "mature" was actually a neon sign shouting their immaturity.

To understand what Paul is saying, we need to consider that he makes this statement at the close of the chapter. Notice how he begins his address in 1 Corinthians 13:

- In verse 1, he says, "If I speak in the tongues of men and of angels, but have not love, I am a noisy gong or a clanging cymbal." All the spiritual disciplines, gifts, and practices in the world are entirely worthless without love.

- In verse 2, he states, "And if I have prophetic powers, and understand all mysteries and all knowledge, and if I have all faith, so as to remove mountains, but have not love, I am nothing." All the knowledge, strength, and power to wow crowds with great wisdom and teaching is worth nothing without love.

- In verse 3, it says, "If I give away all I have, and if I deliver up my body to be burned, but have not love, I gain nothing." Acts of self-sacrifice—be it martyrdom, charitable giving, or dying for the cause of the gospel as a foreign missionary—are entirely worthless without love.

Paul is telling the Corinthian believers that God is not impressed with their spiritual gifts, their knowledge, or their spiritual devotion and obedience. Why? Because they expressed these things not in a self-forgetful, loving way but in a selfish way. Add the Corinthians to the list of people who were corrected in their misguided spiritual efforts.

Because the Christian life is one of faith in Jesus, hope in Jesus, and love for Jesus and everyone he created, the Christian life without love is worthless. We cannot distract ourselves from the centrality of this truth when it comes to our lives in God.

A BEAUTIFUL DEATH

To flesh this out more, let's press into how love is defined in 1 Corinthians 13:4-7 in relation to the two questions that summarize the entire Law (Matt. 22:34-40):

1. What does it mean to love God?
2. What does it mean to love people?

Do you love God with ALL your heart, soul, and mind?

While we could ask you if you have obeyed God's law in every aspect of your life—in thought, word, deed, and intention—since the day you were born (Gal. 3:10), we'd rather ask you a more personal question. Concerning your love for God, do you ever get frustrated with yourself? Are there things about yourself that you really want to change? It is popularly believed that God will remove your struggles if you just have faith, yet this is rarely our experience. We all have things we've longed to be rid of and have asked God to remove, but to no avail. When he does not take these things away, we have to confess that not only do we often get frustrated with him, but we also keep record of the ways he hasn't followed through for us.

We get it. We can honestly say that we too have kept a record against God for things that have or have not happened. In our frustration, we've subtly (or not so subtly) insisted on our own way rather than receiving the life God has given us right now. Instead of loving God as we say we do, we often live in angst over the way he is currently telling his story in our lives; we tend to think he isn't loving because he hasn't changed our predicament. Because of our wrong belief, we fail to love God by keeping a record of the ways we have failed and God has "failed us," and by insisting on our own way ("Take this away, now!"). By the way, we've all sinned in this selfish manner. We usually call it complaining.

Do you love people as you love yourself?

Who comes to mind when you hear, "Do you love people?" Most of us think of all the people we have cozy relationships with, like spouses, kids, friends, parents, siblings, church family, etc. However, the real test of whether or not you love people is not in how you interact with those who do well by you, it's whether or not you have affection for people who don't deliver. What about the people who believe and vote opposite of you? What about the coworker who drives you nuts? What about the people who not only fail you but repeatedly fail you? How are those relationships? Do they still exist or do you keep a record of wrongs? Do you insist on your own way, waiting for them to treat you better? Have you learned how to "just get along" with them, or do you honestly love them?

It's here, face-to-face with our failed performance on just a couple elements of the command to love, that we are forced to admit our ruin. This is why, by God's grace, the Law is also about death—which we define as our total inability to be righteous in and of ourselves and our own efforts.

The Apostle Paul models this death in a very personal way for us in Romans 7:18-20, where he confesses, "For I know that nothing good dwells in me, that is, in my flesh. For I have the desire to do what is right, but not the ability to carry it out." Paul is being shockingly honest here about his own inability. This truth about his weakness causes him to ask the question of questions later in this chapter: "Who will deliver me from this body of death?"

Paul is experiencing first hand the Law's "ministry of death" and "condemnation" (2 Cor. 3:7-9). The Law's gracious ministry is to crush you, condemn you, and bring you to the end of yourself. It's only when we come to the end of ourselves that we can look outside of ourselves. Until then, it's all measuring, mapping, and managing our way through life using our own resources (or even the Scriptures). After all, Paul didn't ask how he could be developed into a better person, but rather, how he could be delivered.

There is much joy in embracing the beautiful death brought to us by the Law. It leads us away from an inward life of self-love, causing us to embrace our total inability and lean on the total ability and faithfulness of Another. Embracing our death pushes us into a life of faith where we welcome the fact that Jesus lived the life of love we couldn't. Jesus was the only One who truly loved God and neighbor. When he died, he died for the dead; and the Father has accepted his death for ours. When he rose, he rose for the dead.

Jesus is our life, and in him, we dwell in perfect obedience to all God has declared. In him, we can walk in the harmony and witness of faith, hope, and love.

THE OLD MAN DIES HARD

As foolish and flawed people, it's easy to use God's grace as a means to do our own thing. "If Jesus already lived a life of faith, obedience, and love for me,. what's the point in me doing these things? Should I not just take the freedom he's given me and do my own thing?" Even if you're not thinking this, if you share the radical message of freedom, sadly, someone will likely assume you are.

This kind of thinking is referred to as "antinomianism." It means a commitment to be lawless and foolish. It's taking the grace of God and using it to live in folly and death.

A friend of mine (Russ) offered a vivid image to describe this life of lawlessness when he said, "Think of it as someone who is down the hall drinking out of a toilet while there is a feast happening in the other room. We are quick to see the folly in that image, and yet, we don't see the folly when we act in the very same way. Like when we refuse to heed the beckoning of our brothers and sisters in an area of our lives. Rather than joining them at the feast of love, we opt to drink from the toilet."

This image resonates with us because, whether verbally or motivationally, we've all exerted our supposed freedom in similar ways. "I'm free to [fill in the blank], you know." Yes, you are free to drink from the toilet, and Jesus will still love you with reckless abandon, but why would you want to? Because as humans, our primary allegiance is to ourselves.

Antinomianism is nothing more than bondage hidden under a veil of freedom. It's here we see that our thirst for control and self-love can express itself in both religious (law-keeping) or irreligious (law-breaking) ways. This is the opposite of dying to ourselves.

We'd rather swing between the extremes of measuring, mapping, and managing than embrace the indignity of indiscriminate grace. We'd rather walk into the Temple with a religious resume or boast to our friends about our irreligious ways than be in the destitute position of the tax collector in Luke 18. Geharde Forde was right: the "old man" dies hard.

WAIT, WATCH & WALK (a joyous way forward)

Enough, already. How does this self-forgetful life of faith, hope, and love express itself?

It makes sense that we would return to the letter of Galatians to find a better and more joyous way forward. It's in Galatians 5:5-6 that Paul helps guide the misguided spiritual efforts of these believers. Notice what he says:

"For through the Spirit, by faith, we ourselves eagerly wait for the hope of righteousness. For in Christ Jesus neither circumcision nor uncircumcision counts for anything, but only faith working through love."

Right off the bat, you'll notice three very familiar words. Faith, hope, and love all appear in these two short verses. Let's examine what Paul is saying here:

Faith = Waiting in dependence on Jesus.

Since Paul already told these believers that "the righteous shall live by faith" in chapter 3 verse 11, it makes sense that he would call them to a life of "waiting" in faith. The word "wait" in Scripture does not mean sitting back and twiddling your thumbs. Instead, it looks like someone eagerly anticipating the arrival of their Uber driver while standing outside a restaurant on a cold January night in Chicago. Waiting is the eager yearning for a God who desires for us to walk in the harmony and witness of love even more than we do.

Hope = Watching for the promise of fruit (righteousness) from Jesus

Instead of running in the manufactured work of our own spiritual sweat and tears, Paul says to wait for the "hope of righteousness." God isn't interested in the fake, plastic nature of manufactured fruit. It has zero value. Instead, he's interested in a true expression of Jesus revealing himself through you in the here and now. Since we have promises like Philippians 1:6—that God will finish the work he began in us—we can watch with hopeful anticipation that Jesus will bear the fruit we long for in his perfect timing (Jn. 15).

Love = Walking in the promised fruit of love from Jesus

Galatians 5:6 says, "For in Christ, neither circumcision nor uncircumcision counts for anything, but only faith working through love." Once again, we find that Paul is not concerned with mere behavior but actions motivated by love. Anything else would be counterfeit change at best. When Jesus follows through on his promise to produce fruit in us, we simply walk in it. This frees us from bitterly seeking to perform spiritually and helps us find the rest Jesus provides, "... my yoke is easy and my burden is light" (Matt 11:28-30).

As illustrated above, the Christian life is one of faith, hope, and love in Jesus. It's a journey of waiting on Jesus to move, watching for where he is at work, and walking in the perfect fruit the Spirit produces as we go. Do not rush into activity. To do so is to trade lawlessness for legalism. The ONLY thing that matters is "faith" expressing itself through "love."

DEPENDENCE-DRIVEN DISCIPLESHIP

In summary, there IS a progression in the Christian life, but it's NOT the upward progression from weakness to strength that's usually presented in Jesus' name. The spiritual progress revealed in the Scriptures is a downward progression from independence to dependence. It's not the ascension of improvement, but the descent into an understanding that we need resurrection.

This is why Jesus held up children as examples of the greatest in his Kingdom. They have no moral resumes to boast of or spiritual prowess to bring to the table. What do they have? Empty hands waiting to be filled and empty mouths waiting to be fed. They are the quintessential models of reception. This example is fitting when you realize that Christ's Kingdom is all about God giving and us receiving, not us accomplishing. It's why Jesus said to a reluctant Peter when attempting to wash his feet, "If I do not wash you, you have no part of me" (Jn. 13:8). Translation: The only way a person experiences Jesus is through being served (Mk. 10:45).

Rather than getting stronger and more competent every day, Christian growth is more about becoming increasingly aware of just how weak and incompetent I am and how strong and competent Jesus was, and continues to be, for me.

Paul Miller, in his book A Praying Life, pointed out the connection between dependence and discipleship when he said, "You don't need self-discipline to pray continuously; you just need to be poor in spirit." This kind of simple, childlike dependence is at the heart of the life God has given us. In fact, when we stop obsessing over our need to get better, that IS what the Bible means by getting better.

The inward infatuation required to "win" in life is the opposite of living a life of faith, hope, and love. It's also exhausting. Donald Miller said it well: "If you want to be viewed as a godly person, at some point you are going to have to start lying." Your social media feed may be filled with quotes of spiritual self-actualization and proof that you're spiritually disciplined, but the yoke of "winning" in the Christian life will eventually wear you down into exhaustion.

In contrast, framing the Christian life in terms of waiting, watching, and walking frees us up to be honest. There's no need to pretend that we're mature or doing better than we actually are. Instead, we can be honest about the ways we see love lacking and how we depend on Jesus to unveil that fruit. And by being honest, we invite others around us to wait, watch, and walk along with us.

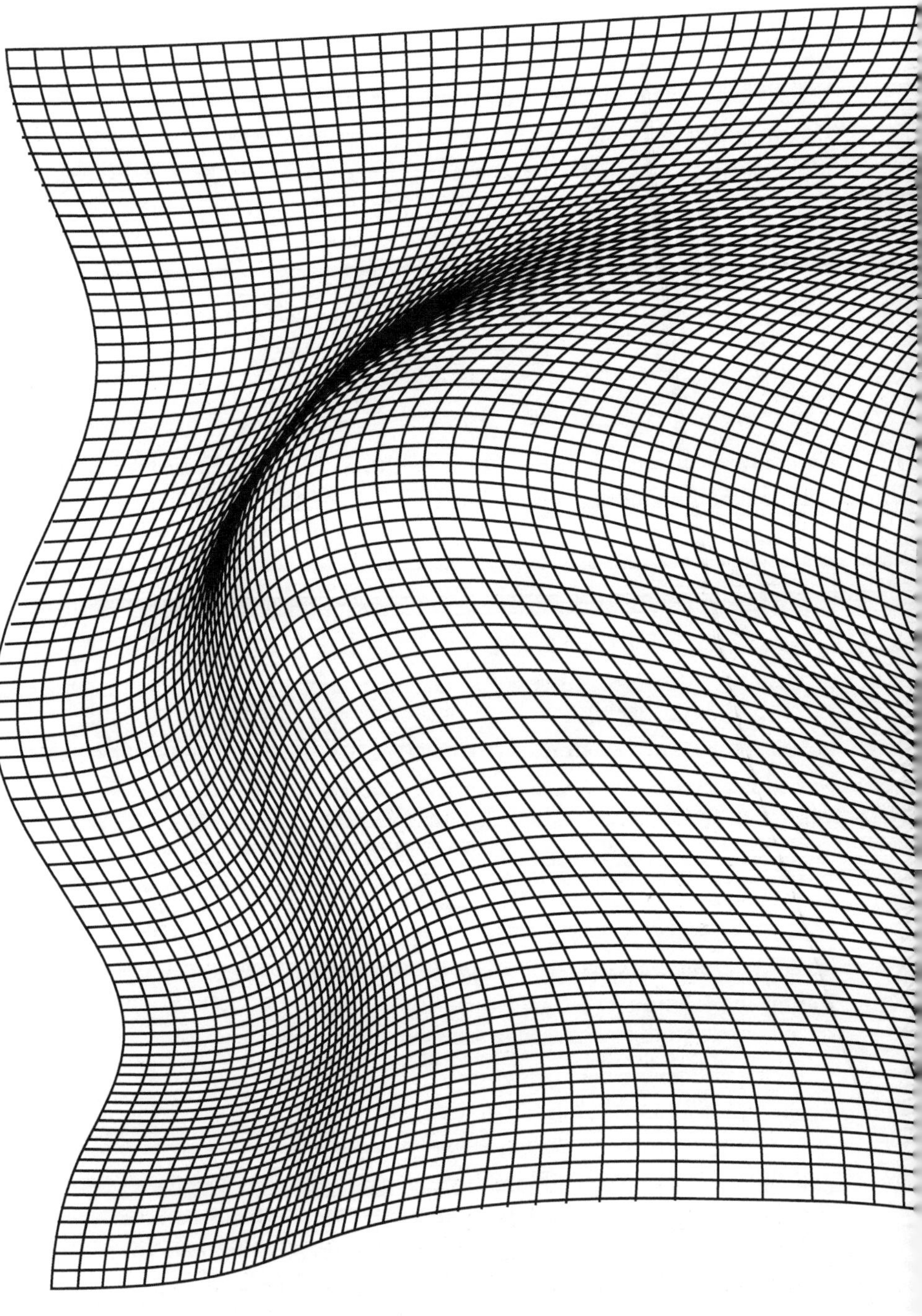

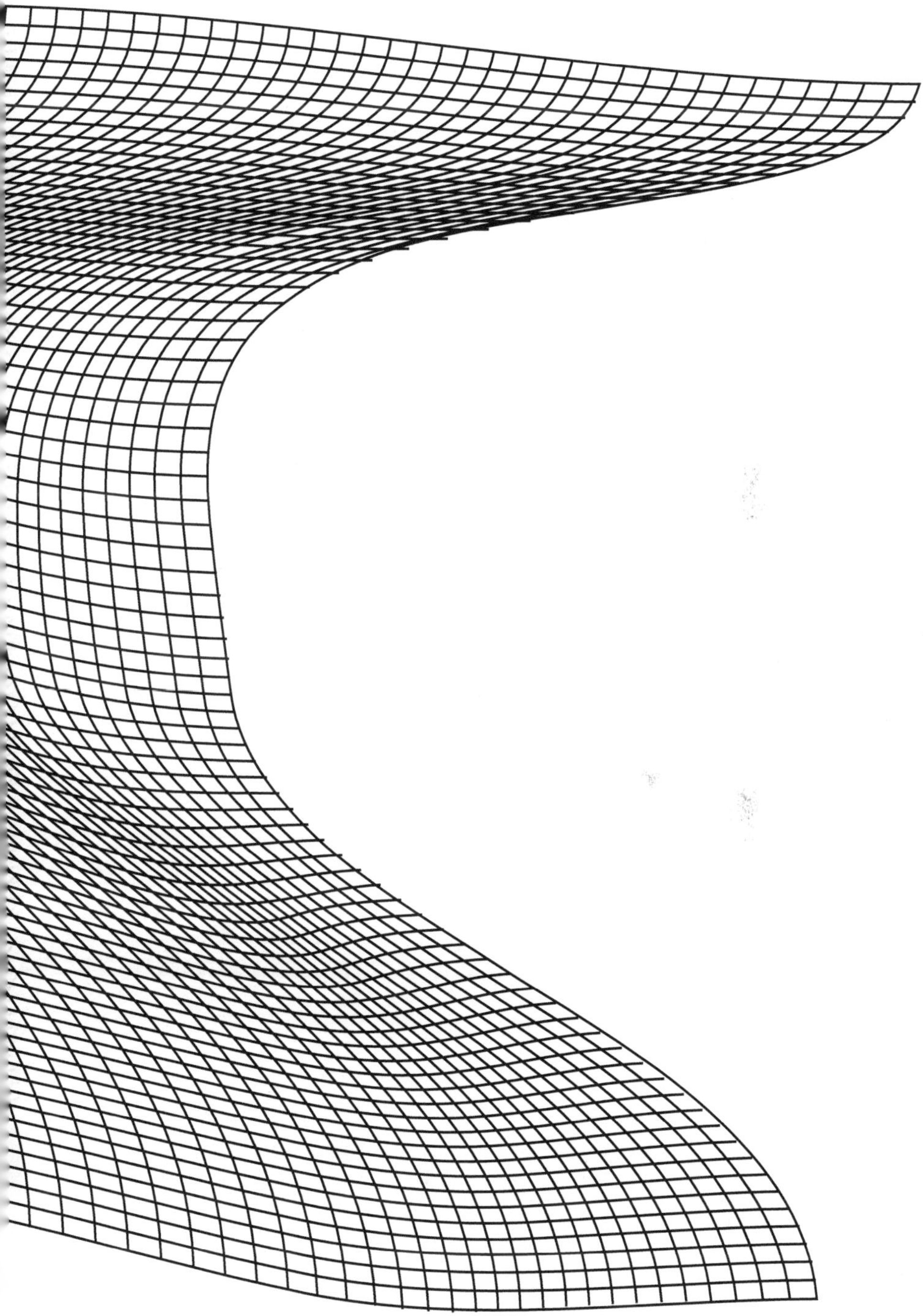

6

RECLAIM 6

CHURCH

Church. Just one of the many words and ideas that has been hijacked in our day. Somewhere along the way, a movement of everyday people defined by indiscriminate grace morphed into a religion, and eventually an institution.

How, in God's name, did this happen?!

Why, after seeing how Jesus came to bring us into harmony with God and all of humanity—so we wouldn't be obsessed over labels—would someone start distracting us from the common solidarity we already have with God and each other—all things having been reconciled?

Why, after watching Jesus embrace outcasts and hearing parables of reckless inclusion—parables that led to the plot and murder of Jesus at the hands of an exclusive religious community—would someone create labels to define who's in and who's out?

The history surrounding these unfortunate shifts will always be discussed and debated. And while we will soon get into some of the details surrounding these changes, discussing how we got here isn't nearly as important as considering the shifts needed to move forward. The critical task at hand in Reclaim 6 is that we reclaim the nature and purpose of the Church as seen in the Scriptures.

JUST WHAT IS THE CHURCH EXACTLY?

Think about the various assumptions packed into the little question, "Where do you go to church?"

The word "church" itself has mistakenly become synonymous with a service we attend (in anywhere from houses to stadiums), the worship styles we practice there, and the leaders who lead it all.

This understanding isn't wrong, like committing an act of sin; but we see it as an unfortunate departure from what the Church was initially intended to be, robbing millions of people along the way from experiencing the fullness of what the Church could be like.

In a day and age where 70 percent (and growing) of society is uninterested in attending a church gathering of any kind, there are unlimited opportunities to meet people right where they're at with the news of God's indiscriminate love. However, we'll never truly be able to experiment with new forms unless we first embrace the freedom we have as the Church.
.

THE NON-RELIGION OF THE PEOPLE
So just what is church exactly?

For too long, people have mislabeled the Church as a "religious institution," but just like Grape-Nuts are not made of either grapes or nuts, the Church is neither a religion nor an institution. The word "church" comes from the Greek word ekklesia—meaning "called-out ones." This term is an unmistakable reference to a group of people, not a place. In other words, it is communal, not institutional. Let us not forget that Jesus died for the world—for people—not for entities, systems, organizational charts or services.

Regarding the Church's unfortunate religious label, let us say this in addition to what you've already read in Reclaim 1 through 5: the essence of any religion is the conditional exchange of acceptance for assimilation. Forgiveness for faithfulness. Religion says, "If you follow the rules, God will love you."

While religion perpetuates the false idea of God as a religious accountant, the Good News is that God already loves the whole world and sent Jesus to prove it (Jn. 3:16). For God so loved the world that he "reconciled us to himself" in the cross of his Son. Whatever needed doing to make peace with sinners, God did all by himself without any human assistance, as we've already seen from Col. 1:19-20.

To reiterate, Paul tells us that Jesus brought peace and unity between God and man. Formerly estranged things are now made right. Enmity is no more, only freedom and friendship.

This wasn't a peace treaty made between two equal parties. God single-handedly reconciled us to himself through the cross of his own Son. A gracious one-sided affair. And the resurrection of Jesus most certainly wasn't the inauguration of a new religion, but rather God's announcement of the end of religion.

As you can see, the church is neither religious nor institutional.

CHURCH AS IDENTITY

If the Church is not a religious institution but a called-out people, then church is first and foremost who we are, not what we do. I want to quickly share a few Scriptures that mention the Church. See if you can't pick up on a theme here:

"Now you are the body of Christ and individually members of it." (1 Cor 12:27)

"There is one body and one Spirit—just as you were called to the one hope that belongs to your call—one Lord, one faith, one baptism, one God and Father of all, who is over all and through all and in all." (Eph 4:4-6)

"So now you Gentiles are no longer strangers and foreigners. You are citizens along with all of God's holy people. You are members of God's family." (Eph. 2:19 NIV)

"... so we, though many, are one body in Christ, and individually members one of another." (Rom. 12:5)

As you can hopefully tell, Scripture's words regarding the Church seem to focus on people and the reality of this new identity they now share by faith in Jesus.

IDENTITY CRISIS

If the pandemic of 2020 (and beyond) has revealed anything about local church expressions in the West, it's that, at our core, we believe we are the Church in our doing. And it has created a bit of an identity crisis.

Somewhere around March of 2020, church gatherings were mandatorily reduced to 250, then to 50, then to 10, and then ultimately discouraged altogether. Church leaders scrambled to move worship experiences from auditoriums to the web and quickly formed teams to encourage and monitor online engagement. Some were happy to still "do church" from their living rooms and were just as happy to post that they had attended #Church from home. Box checked. Still others felt displaced and discouraged because they couldn't "do church" in person. This season unmistakably highlighted our tendency to see church as an activity, not an identity.

But marrying identity to action is a risky business. Who are we when we're at work on Monday instead of worshipping on Sunday? Who are we when we can't gather with our missional communities or serve our neighbors how we had imagined because of a pandemic? Who are we when we don't hit ALL the supposed "marks" of a faithful church expression? Does it "count" as church to dive into spiritual conversation and prayer on a Thursday night with our spouse, children, or friends? Are everyday people free to create new faith communities for those they love?

We wrestle with questions like this because we rarely get to the heart of the matter: our identity. In a time of deconstruction, reimagination, preservation, and innovation, people are obsessed with what should or should not "count" as church. But taking our freedom seriously removes "counting" altogether, allowing us to see that, in Jesus' name, everything counts (Col. 3:17).

THE IMPACT OF THE TEMPLE

You might be wondering—like us—how we got from the simplicity and freedom of Jesus' body in the world to the complexity and busyness of what masquerades as church today. While most point a finger at the Roman Emperor Constantine as the godfather of this modern ecclesial dilemma, it seems that our love affair with structures we can control goes back farther than 312 AD.

Maybe you've heard of the Temple in Jerusalem and the king who built it. His name was Solomon. For Israel, the decision to build the Temple was much like the decision to become a monarchy. Neither was God's idea. The Temple project was the brainchild of King David (and was built by Solomon seven years later), and God made it known to David that He never asked for it to be built. He told David through the prophet Nathan, "Wherever I have moved with all the Israelites, did I ever say to any of their rulers whom I commanded to shepherd my people Israel, 'Why have you not built me a house of cedar?'" (2 Samuel 7:7).

God seemed content to dwell in the temporary tent known as the tabernacle. Perhaps this was due to its simplicity and mobility. Everything about the tabernacle was simple. It was constructed of linen curtains, goat hair curtains, and wood. Because it was always on the move, it was often in need of repair, and that was okay.

God chose Israel as a nation of people through whom to reveal himself, but he never intended to exclude other nations in the process. God's heart was always to bless all nations so that all people could experience the freedom and family found only through him (Gen. 12:3b). The tabernacle, like Israel, was a divine means to a divine end, and the simplicity and mobility of the tabernacle allowed it to fulfill its purpose. In contrast, the temple was an extravagant and permanent structure that was unnecessary.

By the time of Jesus, the Temple had been rebuilt by King Herod. For the religious of the day, the Temple (and the ceremonies held within it) unequivocally represented God's presence and were the only means to connect with him and be assured of atonement (forgiveness). Jesus was constantly ruffling religious feathers by challenging, among other things, Israel's misconceptions of the Temple. He flat-out declared that he was greater than the Temple (Matt. 12:6-8), hinted at its unimportance (Jn. 2:18-22), and predicted its destruction (Matt. 24:1-2). This perceived lack of respect for the Temple led to the plot to kill Jesus.

Based on 1 Peter 2:4-5 and Ephesians 2:21, we know that God never intended for David's model of a physical temple to be the standard pattern for how the Church positions itself and functions in the world. An entire nation thought that one specific building, in one particular city, could fulfill God's plan to "bless all nations." In contrast, the Church is referred to as "living stones...

being built up as a spiritual house" and a "holy priesthood." We were always meant to be a defined people, scattered throughout the world, who carry the Good News of Jesus' finished work to all people in all places. No wonder Jesus did the majority of his ministry outside the Temple and seemed unconcerned about its destruction.

Although the Temple was destroyed in 70 AD as Jesus had predicted, the same impulse that led to its construction is still alive and well today. And while some are content to embrace the status quo, others are continually embattled in efforts to reform the Church.

We've lived on both ends of the spectrum and have decided to embrace what the Church is according to the Scriptures: A liberated people trusting in God's indiscriminate grace.

FUNCTIONING AS THE CHURCH

It is a beautiful thing when this global community marked by faith alone (the Church) begins to embrace our identity and the freedom that gives shape to our life together—a life we can freely live regardless of the day, time, or location.

In Galatians 5:1, Paul says, "For freedom Christ has set us free, stand firm therefore, and do not submit again to a yoke of salvery." He's talking to a group of believers who have brushed up against the kind of leader that lays spiritual burdens on people—the kind that encourages people to labor so they can maintain their status as a "church member in good standing." But Paul says that we are now free. Free to rest in a love that will not quit on us and free to live out the New Testament vision for Jesus' body.

In our freedom we:

Greet one another (Rom. 16:16), offer hospitality to one another (1 Pet. 4:9), and welcome one another because Christ has freely welcomed us (Rom. 15:7).

Bear with one another (Col. 3:13), are kind to one another, are tenderhearted, and forgive one another because God in Christ has forgiven us (Eph. 4:32).

Submit to one another (Eph. 5:21) and show humility toward one another (Phil. 2:3) because Jesus submitted to the will of the Father and humbled himself to the point of death, even death on a cross (Phil. 2:8).

Serve one another (Gal. 5:13) because Christ came not to be served, but to serve (Mk. 10:45).

Confess our own brokenness to one another and pray for one another (Jas. 5:16) because Jesus is our righteousness (2 Cor. 5:21), and as our mediator and intercessor, Jesus' blood cleanses us from all sin (1 Jn 1:7).

Live in harmony (Rom. 12:16) and peace (Mk. 9:50) with one another because we have peace with God through our Lord Jesus Christ (Rom. 5:1).

Care for one another (1 Cor. 12:25) and carry one another's burdens (Gal. 6:2) because Jesus bore our sin burden in his body on the cross (1 Pet. 2:24).

Weep and rejoice with one another (Rom. 12:15) because Jesus is a sympathetic Savior (Heb. 4:15) and our true reason to rejoice (1 Pet. 1:8).

Honor one another (Rom. 12:10) and count others as more significant than ourselves (Phil. 2:3) because Christ made himself nothing (Phil. 2:7).

Love one another because he first loved us (1 Jn. 4:19).

As you ponder these verses, think about how Jesus embodied these things in the various spaces in which he found himself. These things happened over meals, in homes, around fires, on beaches, during festivals, on walks, in boats, in the morning, and at night—not primarily in synagogues or in the Temple. As people who live in Jesus—his body in the world—we are free to walk in these acts as we relate to one another and live out the purpose he has given us as his Church.

THE MINISTRY & MESSAGE OF THE RECONCILED

In the introduction to this book, we quoted Rachel Held Evans' description of the Church of Jesus as "a bunch of outcasts and oddballs gathered at a table, not because they are rich or worthy or good, but because they said yes [to Jesus] …

And there's always room for more."

These words are powerful, prophetic, and echo the behavior of the ancient Church. Of course, we're referring to the New Testament version that existed prior to any Orthodox or Catholic versions, but I digress. This quote from Evans brings us back to the original question at the heart of Reclaim 6: what is the identity and purpose of the Church?

First, we are objects of God's reconciling love, just like our unbelieving neighbors. By faith, however, we happen to be in on the Good News before some of the others. Second, since we know that God is love, we carry and proclaim this distinct message to the world.

God cares so much about the whole world that he baked the ministry and message of this cosmic reconciliation right into the Church's purpose.

According to 2 Corinthians 5:18-19: "God... gave us the ministry of reconciliation." And "God... entrust[ed] to us the message of reconciliation."

In a day and age where the idea of church has been reduced to buildings labeled as "churches" and the services held within, we come to find out that the Church is none other than the "called-out ones"—those sent to be a constant sign to the whole world that they too have been reconciled and called out of their unbelief. This proclamation of grace is what makes the Church the Church.

Please note: this message has been entrusted to the people known as the Church, not events mistaken for church. While it's quite alright to peg one gifted person as the mouthpiece for a whole group, the fact remains that:

1. 2 Corinthians 5 tells us that we have all been given this message.
2. Most of our friends aren't willing to attend a church event and listen to people they don't know.
3. The early Church grew from 120 people gathered in an upper room in Jerusalem to a global community because everyday, unnamed people shared the message.

In other words, the Church is defined by what it declares. And what we declare is, "IT IS FINISHED." Even in its unbelief, the world is no less embraced by the reconciliation that God brought to the world than we are. There are no "ins" and "outs," just those who are enjoying the mystery of Christ and others who are still ignorant of it or flat-out refuse to join the party (i.e., the older brother in Lk. 15).

But regardless of the position or beliefs of those around us, the Church exists to be tangibly FOR THE WORLD. What else could Paul mean by "ministry of reconciliation"? Declaring the reality of this reconciliation—that the work is finished—within growing friendships is the ministry Jesus has called us into.

THE FREEDOM OF THE FREE

In a community where Jesus is our righteousness, there is no need to pretend we have our lives together. By faith in what Jesus has accomplished on the cross, the Church was, and is today, the one community where it's okay to be broken, weak, doubting, discouraged, angry, depressed, hurting, and flawed because we already stand holy in him (Heb. 10:10). In Jesus, we are free to confess our frailty and free to leave the exhausting madness of trying to hide the junk in our lives, just as we are free to humbly receive the encouragement of a brother or sister who reminds us of the Person and promises of Jesus.

People may be inspired for a short while by stories of heroism and hard work, but sharing hope from the vantage point of need, frailty, and the brokenness we all share is where true breakthrough occurs. Being honest about the messy parts of our lives, however, requires genuine security—a type of security only spawned by knowing you're held by a love that will never let you go.

But living and posturing ourselves in this way will never happen until we take seriously the freedom we already have in Jesus. Until we see and believe that we already are the Church because of what Jesus has done and declared, we will remain tethered to ideas of church that limit what could be in the name of ministry.

Only in discovering and believing that being the Church is first an identity, not an activity, will we find the freedom to join our neighbors in their celebrations and cry with them through their pains. Only here, in this freedom, will we find the courage to position ourselves as the "outcasts and oddballs" we indeed are. Only radical freedom will give way to us slowing down so we can tell others of the One who has set us free. May it be so.

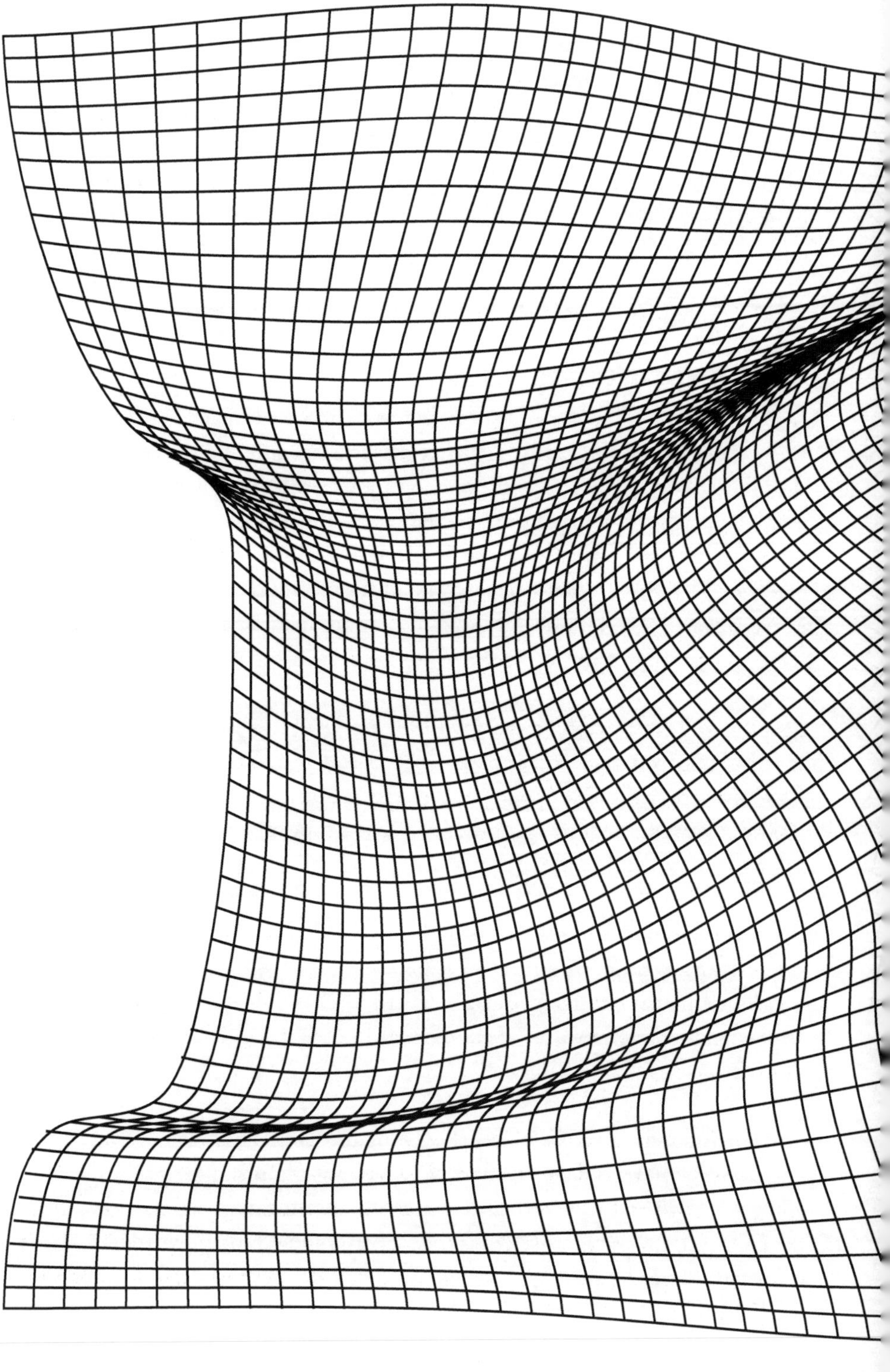

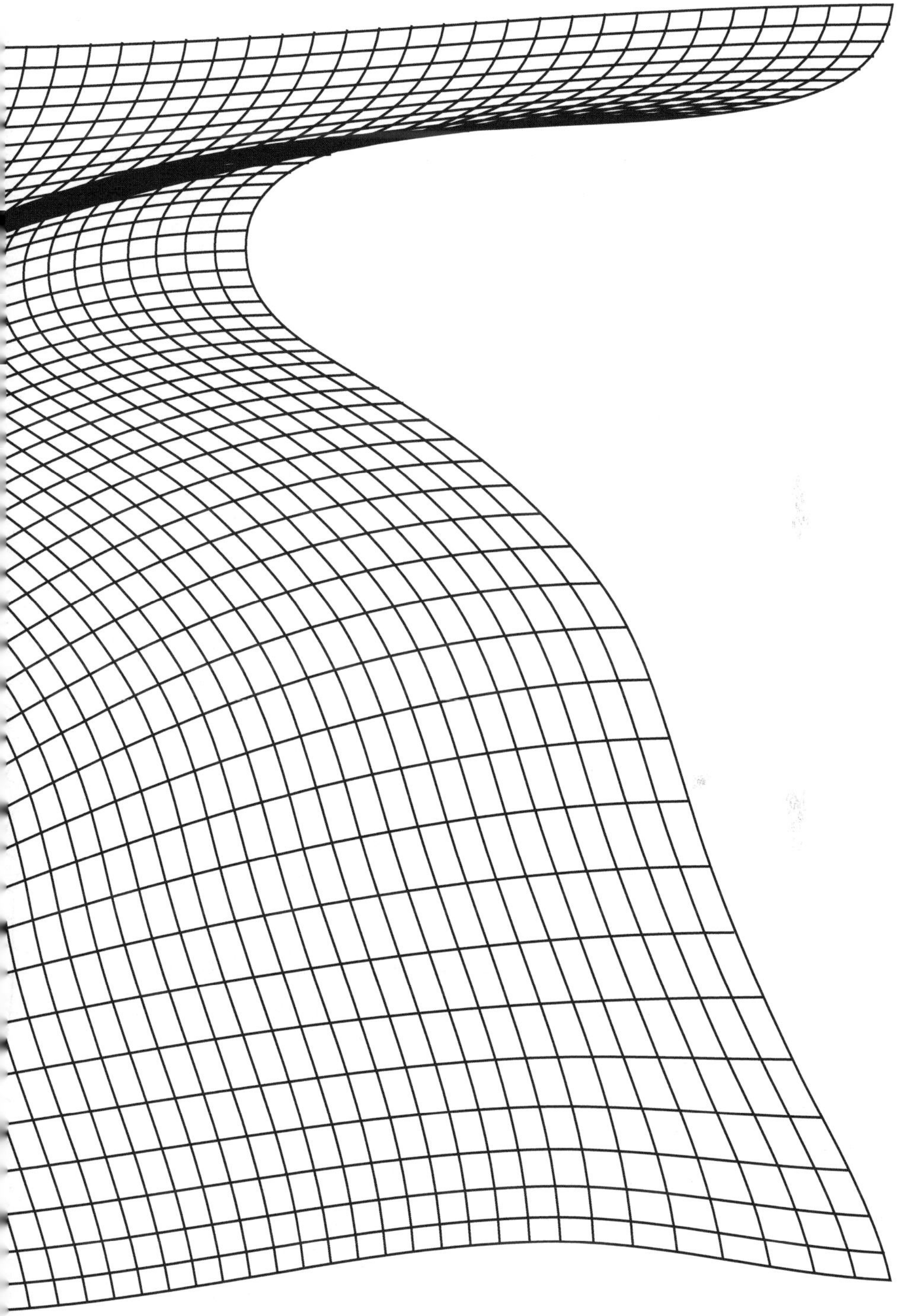

7

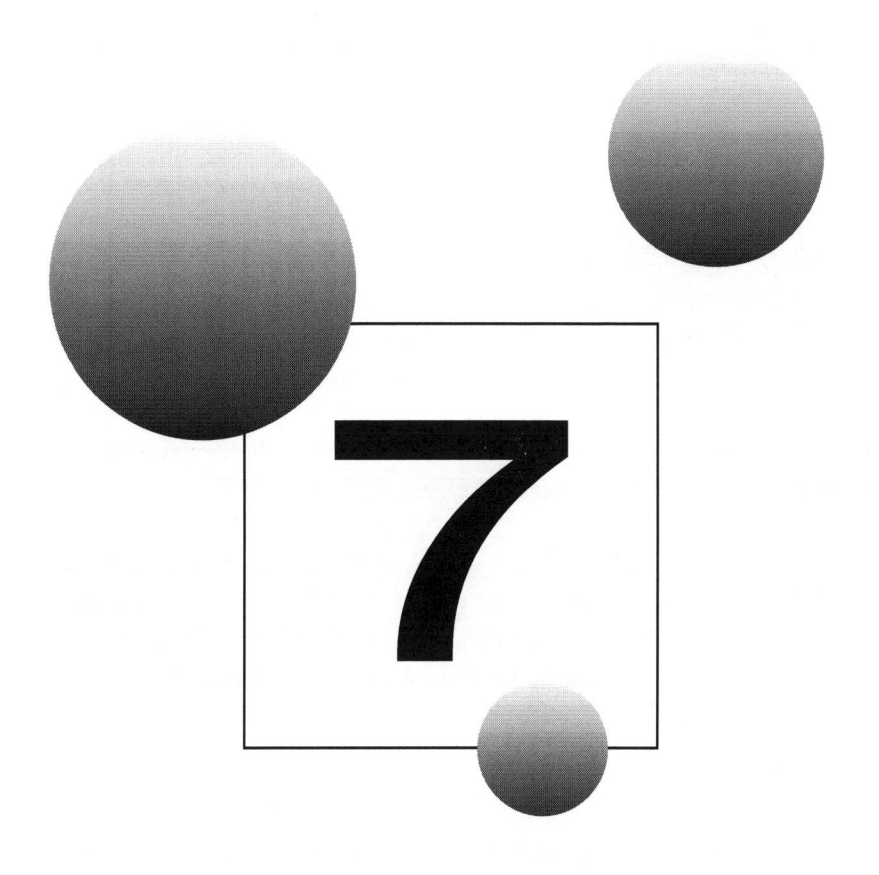

RECLAIM 7

DISCIPLESHIP

There's been a considerable amount of ink spilled on the topic of discipleship in recent years. If you've been in and around this conversation, chances are you've had your fill of alliterated paradigms, leadership principles, and missional geometry. While a great deal of the thinking and writing on the topic of discipleship has been helpful, some has served to complicate matters or, even worse, add pressure and performance to something that should otherwise be a source of joy in our lives.

The same Jesus who offers rest also sends us into the world as missionaries (Jn. 20:21). We've already seen how these two things are closely connected in the Scriptures. In the following pages, we will unpack why discipleship is best defined by friendship, along with what that means and why it matters today.

TWO SHIFTS

When you look at the Jerusalem of 2,000 years ago, you find a city plagued with various forms of religion. Even the good, gracious Law given by God to Israel was perverted by Israel's spiritual leadership, causing fear, guilt, and burn-out (Matt. 11:28-30). Naturally, it wouldn't make sense for another movement in God's name to explode on the scene and impact 65 percent of the Roman Empire in less than 300 years. Yet, that is exactly what happened.

The question for our consideration is — how did it happen?

First, there was a shift in what was being *said*. The cross of Christ wasn't a declaration of a new religion. Instead, it was the announcement that God has left the religion business altogether, solving all the world's problems without a shred of religious effort on anyone's part. As Robert Capon put it, "In Jesus, God has put up a 'Gone Fishing' sign on the religion shop. He has done the whole job in Jesus once and for all and simply invited us to believe it." This message was a complete shift in everything the world had ever heard in the name of God.

Second, there was a shift in what was being *done*. By faith, those who believed in Jesus became a family and began functioning as a family, both in their relationship with God and with others (see Reclaim 6). These everyday people—known as the Church—went from caring for each other to loving, encouraging, and welcoming strangers to the table. While other groups existed for their own glory and what they could gain in this life, this liberated movement of people existed solely for the good of those around them.

EVERYDAY PEOPLE EXTENDING WHAT THEY ENJOY

Connecting our experiences to the life Jesus has invited us into is essential. This helps safeguard against the performance and pressure felt all too often in the "missional" conversations of our day.

You may have heard us talk about the connection between enjoying and extending before. It's a human phenomenon that plays out around the globe in every culture and tribe. Be it a rare barrel-aged stout, an oceanside view, or an addictive new show—we all naturally extend to others the things we enjoy.

Consider how this relates to discipling others. As referenced in Reclaim 6, 2 Corinthians 5:18 tells us, "All this is from God, who through Christ reconciled us to himself and gave us the ministry of reconciliation."

This invitation to extend the Good News—God's gracious work of reconciling broken people (the only kind of people there are) to himself—is a matter of offering to others what we have already experienced and enjoy. The "ministry of reconciliation" is not like a telemarketing job—cold calling people to sell (from a script) services and products you most likely don't even use or benefit from. Rather, God is inviting the reconciled to share the good news of reconciliation.

From the man born blind to the woman at the well, from the demoniac to the cripple at the Beautiful Gate—this news of reckless love spreads throughout society by means of discipleship, carried out by every believer who has experienced it's healing and reconciling power.

And because almost all of the growth we see in the New Testament came by way of unimpressive and often unnamed individuals, we can be confident that Jesus' plan is still the spread of his Church under the leadership of everyday people. He is using students and CEOs, singles and stay-at-home moms, farmers and freelancers, physicians and pub owners alike in the unfolding of his Kingdom.

THE WORK OF DISCIPLESHIP IN A SCRIPTURAL CONTEXT

In reclaiming this ancient practice of discipleship, we have found value in looking at the details surrounding Jesus' words in Matthew 28 as we seek to introduce God's reckless grace to a religious world. Going forward, we will be taking a deeper look at two things: (1) the mission Jesus has brought us into, and (2) the society we find ourselves in today.

1) Understanding Our Mission

Take a minute to read Matthew 28:18-20. The first thing Bible scholars will tell you to do when you encounter the word "therefore," is ask yourself the question, "What is 'therefore' there for?" The answer is found in the preceding verse where Jesus reminds his disciples that all authority has been given to him in heaven and on earth. In the same manner, Jesus made this chosen group of ragtag witnesses the carriers of his message, and he authorized them to "disciple."

Although it is widely agreed upon that the call of Jesus is paramount in these verses, there is often confusion as to what exactly he commissioned his followers to do. "Go and make disciples of all nations" can be read a couple different ways. The standard approach has a bent towards being sent to other nations to make disciples. However, there are several reasons why this reading is problematic. A clearer understanding of this passage will help us see this mission as something for both our neighborhoods and other nations.

The difficulty in taking a standard approach to Matthew 28 occurs primarily because of the two verbs present in the passage: "go" and "make." Let's start with "go." (Brace yourself—this is a bit of necessary grammar talk). Verbs come in two common forms: infinitive and participle. So for our example, the verb would be either "go" (infinitive) or "going" (participle). Most Bible translations render the word as "go," although the Greek word in the original text is a participle. It should read "going" or "as you are going."

The other issue is the phrase "make disciples," and this is more of a theological dilemma. If someone is commanded to make disciples, the implication is that it is in their power to make that happen. However, as we interpret Scripture with Scripture, we find that the One who makes disciples is God himself; we simply point people to him. The resolution here is to see the verb phrase "make disciples" as the "act of discipling" (as in, "I disciple Joe"). Although God is the One who makes disciples, the commission here to disciple people uses the imperative verb in the original text. "Go, disciple people!"

By putting both of these ideas together, the rendering of this passage becomes, "Therefore, as you are going, disciple people of all nations, baptizing them..."

With this reading, the pressure of the command to go is lifted and replaced with the natural organic flow of moving through life, watching for the Spirit-led opportunity to DISCIPLE! This translation removes the tendency to compartmentalize work, family, and ministry. It weaves the mission of discipling through all of life organically.

But if our mission is to "disciple," then what do we do with the work of evangelism?

Neil Cole has pointed out that at some point in the past, the Church created a separation in what it means to "disciple," labeling one camp Evangelism and the other Discipleship—often creating two different departments in the church known as Outreach and Teaching. To correct this misunderstanding, we must note that the Greek word evangelion isn't an "ism." It's not something we do, but instead something we share, as the word literally means "good news." In short, to evangelize is simply to proclaim the Good News of Jesus to those we love and meet along life's path.

Most haven't stopped to consider that most of the New Testament mentions of the gospel are written and applied to communities of people who already believe.

It's not accurate to view the gospel as a message strictly intended to be an entry point for those who don't yet believe, while thinking something else is needed for those who do. Tim Keller says it well:

> The gospel is not just for non-Christians, but also for Christians. This means the gospel is not just the A-B-C's but the A to Z of the Christian life. It is not accurate to think 'the gospel' is what saves non-Christians, and then, what matures Christians is trying hard to live according to Biblical principles. It is more accurate, according to Scripture, to say that we are saved by believing the gospel, and then we are transformed in every part of our mind, heart, and life by believing the gospel more and more deeply as our life goes on. [1]

MOVING FORWARD

In light of the meaning unveiled in the words of Jesus in Matthew 28 and the discipleship efforts we see throughout the New Testament, we believe discipleship is best defined as "good news shared through friendships." We see five elements at work within these friendships and conversations, all of them undergirded by a trust in the Spirit to produce fruit. Knowing how to disciple someone, and growing in that knowledge, is important—but none of us is the Christ or the Spirit he sent into the world. The Spirit is a much better disciple-maker than any system or process. Therefore, we trust him to produce fruit when and how he chooses.

What does it look like to pass on good news through the simple art of friendship?

- *Being present* with the people in our lives
- *Listening* to the people we are discipling
- *Sharing* the person and promises of Jesus in light of where people are
- *Inviting* people to trust Jesus, to take him at his word
- *Teaching* people to wait, watch, and walk in the fruit the Spirit produces

---

1 http://bit.ly/keller-preaching-the-gospel-in-a-postmodern-culture

5 DISCIPLESHIP BASICS

Being Present
Intentionally Showing Up

While it may seem redundant to say we should be present with the people we are discipling, it needs to be said. Intentionally showing up in people's lives is an often overlooked component of discipleship. "The Word became flesh and dwelt among us" (Jn. 1:14) is not merely a poetic turn of phrase—it's a demonstration of the incarnational and intentional love of God who came to live, laugh, love, work, slow down, eat, and converse among us. Because we live in him (Gal. 2:20), we are ambassadors of Jesus (2 Cor. 5:20) who incarnate this way of life among the people in our lives. We are present among people. We intentionally show up for their sake, ready, willing, and able to listen to them, serve them, and proclaim Good News.

Listening
Understanding the Stories

Because adults learn on a need-to-know basis, there's simply no way to disciple someone "where they are" if you don't first, well, know where they are. Those who slow down with others to hear their stories will, over time, find out where people uniquely are in their journeys. By listening, you'll discover what they celebrate and what they struggle with. Eventually, as trust builds, people will begin to share all they've seen, heard, and done in the name of God and Church and will be interested in your input. But it all starts with listening. At every turn and in every place, we see Jesus pointing to truths that stem from what he heard people were wrestling with. He knew where they were and simply met them there.

Sharing
Speaking Truth & Grace Into the Stories

Being present and listening. These are two surefire components of any loving relationship, and they are non-negotiables when it comes to discipling those around you. Once someone has shared an aspect of their story, you then have the opportunity to share a part of your story that connects with theirs. It's here that people can see you're just like them. It's here that you can share what God has shown and taught you in light of the topics and issues at hand. And it's here that those who aren't ready for "meat" (a look at the Scriptures) can be discipled right where they are with "milk" (the truth and grace of Jesus in your story).

Inviting
Encouraging Belief in Light of Where They Are

When someone hears the good news of Jesus, they often wonder about their next step. Instead of shying away from this conversation, help them process what they are thinking and feeling in light of the conversation you're having. For some, the next step will be to continue the conversation—maybe even begin pressing further into the Scriptures. Others may need to consider what their lives and situations would look like if what you're sharing about Jesus were true. Some, after being convinced of the truths you're sharing about Jesus, will wonder how to begin acting on these things. Regardless of where they are on their faith journey, the invitation is always to trust Jesus.

Teaching
Helping People to Wait, Watch & Walk

In Matthew 28:20, Jesus said, "... [teach] them to observe all that I have commanded..." Understanding this helps us make a shift in our discipleship efforts—from teaching people what Jesus has done to helping them see life through the lens of what he has declared. It's a process of meeting them where they are and looking to what God has said. It's teaching them to WAIT on the Spirit as they seek Jesus, WATCH for where he is at work, and WALK in the fruit the Spirit produces in their lives (see Reclaim 5 for more on this).

ADDING TRUST TO THE EQUATION

While these discipleship basics are as relevant as ever—and there has never been a greater need for non-programmatic discipleship—you and I are still just guests at the table Jesus has prepared for us all. Trusting the King of the Kingdom enables us to play the long game in our relationships with those disinterested, dismissed, dissed, and run-down by the Church. Belief and trust in the one and only true missional community at work in this world (the Trinity) helps us to be okay with moving at the speed of his timetable—not ours.

This trust enables us to take our eyes off ourselves and helps create an atmosphere of ease and lightness with others—the kind of calm and chill Jesus displayed when he was hanging out at the party at Matthew's house (Matthew 9:10).

Referring to discipleship relationships, a friend of mine (Russ) once said: "We trip into the mystery of a certain Someone (Jesus) in someone else's life and play along." Trusting allows us to move at the speed of Jesus in the lives of others. There's really no other speed at which to move if you think about it.

THE WORK OF DISCIPLESHIP IN A SOCIAL CONTEXT

1) Understanding Society

Over the years, many strides have been taken to see the gospel spread and lives changed, especially in areas such as music, design, teaching, architecture, literature, and the use of technology. We are grateful for the many servants who have poured into these areas of ministry. However, after all the countless hours spent on books, blogs, and conferences, the Church in the West continues to shrink in numbers and influence.

According to research conducted in North America by Barna, Pew, Lifeway, and others, 70 percent of society is uninterested in attending a church service of any kind. [2] There is even evidence that this number has increased to 80 percent post-Covid. [3] Also, 36 percent of 15-30 years old (Millennials) have no spiritual interest and have been labeled as the spiritual "nones." [4] This is the largest recorded percentage of spiritual disinterest among a generation in U.S. history leading to the lowest recorded percentage of in-house church memberships. [5] To top it all off, we recently learned that less than 20 percent of churchgoers have heard of and can articulate what is classically known as the "Great Commission." [6]

---

2 http://bit.ly/lifeway-research-unchurched-will-talk-about-faith-not-interested-in-going-to-church
3 http://bit.ly/barna-new-sunday-morning-part-2
4 http://bit.ly/pew-research-religious-composition-of-younger-millennials
5 http://bit.ly/us-church-membership-falls-below-majority-for-first-time
6 http://bit.ly/half-churchgoers-not-heard-great-commission

Take a moment to consider what this means. The primary platform the Church uses to connect with people doesn't interest 80 percent of the population. And the primary people involved in discipling an uninterested world make up less than 20 percent of the Church.

When considering how people outside the institutional church are engaging in faith conversations and spiritual friendships, we should take into account some other social phenomena. Listed below are three cultural realities affecting most people in the world:

- *Covid-19:* The pandemic that started in 2020 is still lingering at the time this book is being written. We have no idea what the long-term ramifications of this cultural moment will be. We've seen how the arrival of this virus, and the subsequent global response, has upset the rhythms and lives of individuals, families, communities, and businesses. For now, it's changed the way we shop, work, entertain ourselves, eat, travel, learn, and connect.

- *Social Media:* Speaking of connection! People long for human connection, so it's only fitting that millions of people are trying to find it through several online platforms: Instagram, Twitter, Reddit, Pinterest, SnapChat, TikTok, Clubhouse, Facebook, etc.

- *Cultural Fragmentation:* Because more and more people are moving away from home and settling in cities for school and careers, cities are no longer as homogeneous as they once were. Instead, society is divided into many distinct subcultures that are connected through common interests, socio-economic status, lifestyle, etc. For instance, the Ukrainian Village, a neighborhood in Chicago that got its name from the immigrants who settled it, is now made up of young urban professionals from every background and town in the Midwest.

We can point to two primary impacts social media and cultural fragmentation have made on society as a whole:

- *Relational Void:* Connection and real community are two different things, which is why those who are connected to others online still hunger for real-life relationships that involve time, space, and face-to-face interaction.

The connection/community distinction is also why there were multiple reports of people feeling lonely, depressed and even harboring thoughts of suicide as they were asked to shelter in place during the COVID-19 pandemic—even though many of these same people were using social and video platforms more than ever.

- *Rise Of Tribes:* The "neighborhood" has been the traditional social unit of society until recently. The cultural realities previously discussed have given rise to what Seth Godin refers to as "tribes." These affinity-based circles are where people are finding community and living life. There is seemingly a tribe for every interest, activity, life philosophy, and passion.

WHAT IT ALL MEANS

What do these trends mean for the way people approach faith today? For those who did not inherit a sense of faith from their upbringing, it means that they will likely approach their faith journey within friendships—giving a listening ear only to those they know and trust. In light of this, one implication for the social path to faith rises to the top: Providing people with a place to belong on their way to belief.

Evangelistic services and popular speakers don't have the same pull to make a person rethink their beliefs as they once did. Sure, they often have an impact for good on those undergoing a personal crisis, but not so much with the many who feel "good to go" in life. To offer the friendships people need, we will need to remember that: (1) Jesus used the word "net" to describe the Kingdom of God in Matthew 13:47-50; (2) this particular word describes a very specific dragnet that indiscriminately grabs every single thing in its path (bones, old boots, beer cans, and... well, you name it.) (3) Jesus said that the contents of the net would not be separated until the net reaches the shore; and (4) he made it clear that the job of separating falls to his department—not ours.

With this reality in mind, we are free to be who we really are: people in the net who befriend others in the net, just as they are. With nothing more to prove or accomplish than the beer-can floating alongside us, we are free to *be present* with others as we *listen* to their stories, *share* good news, *invite* them to trust in what Jesus has done, and *teach* them to to walk in what he's doing.

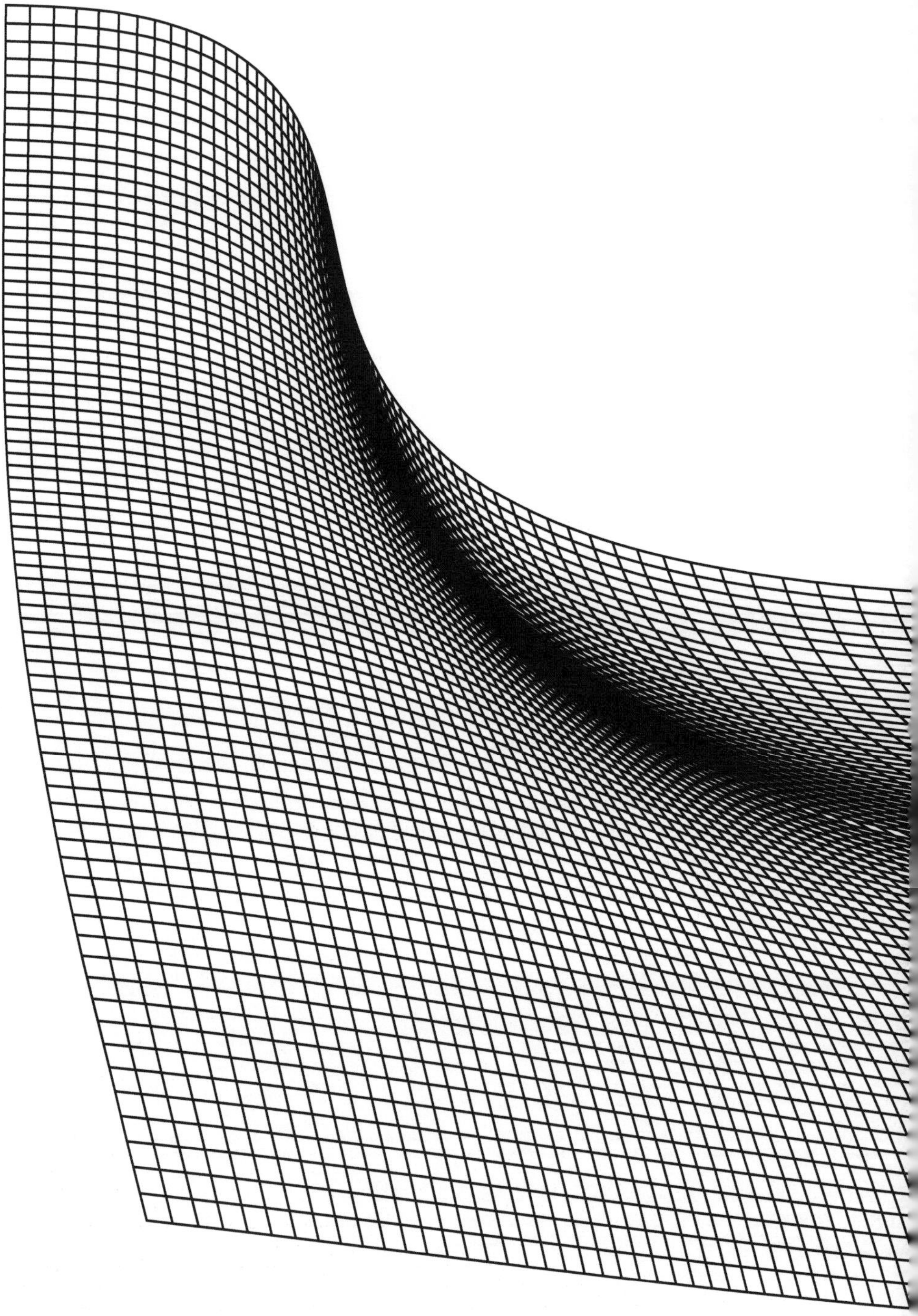

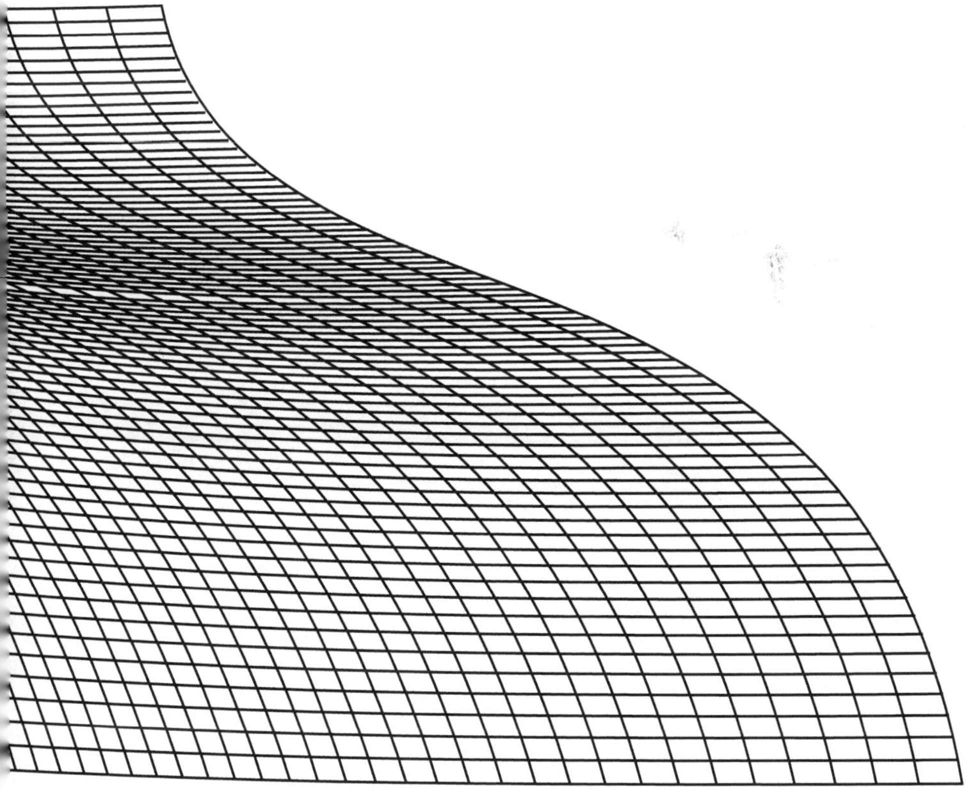

8

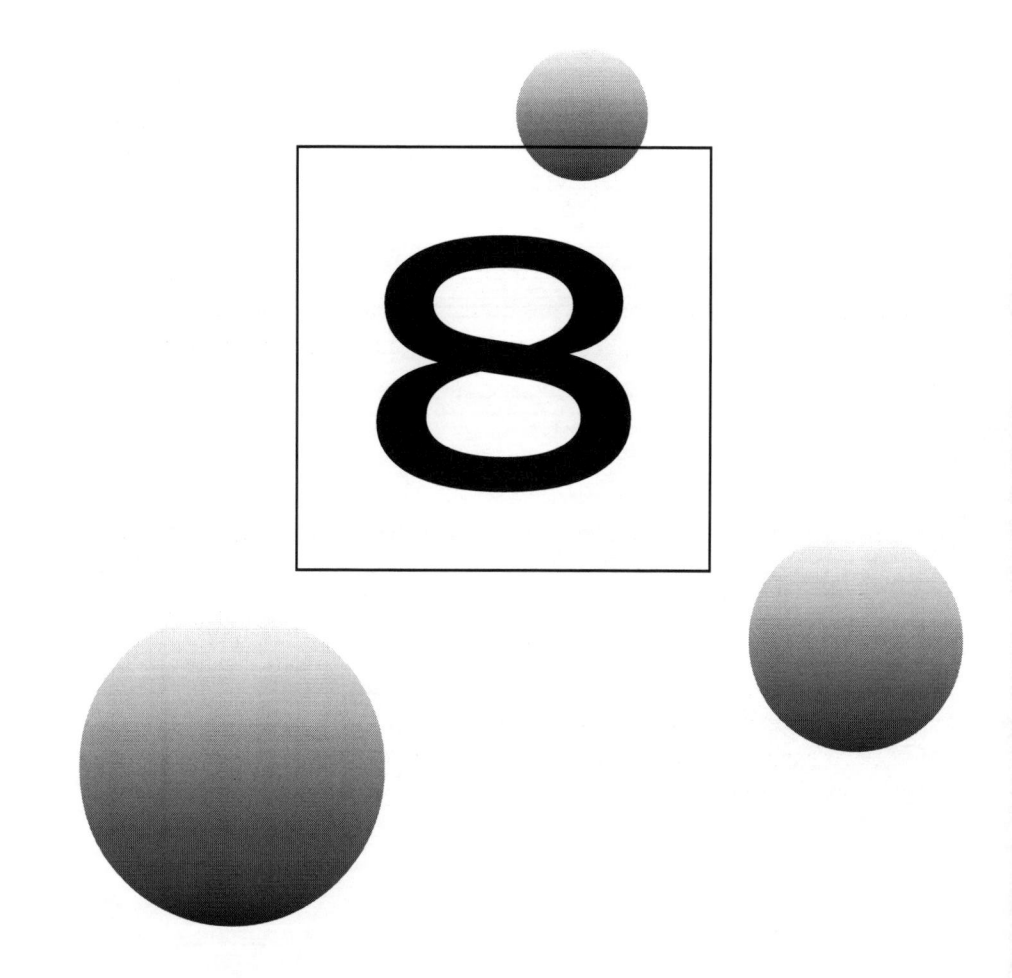

RECLAIM 8

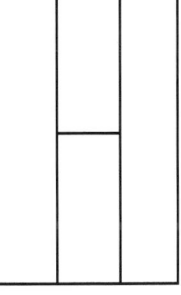

SPACES

In Reclaim 6, we took a look at the Church's identity (i.e., a liberated people) and introduced its purpose in the world (i.e., to carry the message of reconciliation). In Reclaim 7, we dove into what this ministry of reconciliation tangibly looks like as we unpacked the word "discipleship."

With this as our backdrop, Reclaim 8 is about how you can spend your time passing on good news and encouraging others who are doing the same. In short, how you can go about being the Church in the world—which is easy to complicate.

A HARD LESSON LEARNED
In 2010, my family and I (Russ) moved from Asheville, NC, to Chicago to make disciples and plant churches. Upon entering a major city that was reportedly 80 percent unchurched, I was determined to make a shift in how we functioned as a local church. For this shift, I looked to Jesus as the template for a new approach.

With Jesus himself as our foundation, we launched "missional communities." These new communities sought to cultivate rhythms, helping people to pattern their lives after our missional God. We also built a system aimed at providing leaders with ongoing instruction and accountability.

Was it simple? Yes.
Was it biblical? Yes.
Was it successful? Yes.
Was it effective? Yes.
Was it freeing? No.

We were very effective at helping people form new rhythms, and we multiplied over fifty missional communities. We even planted churches from these communities. We did it so well that other pastors were calling and asking us to train them to do the same thing in their context.

However, as people inevitably failed to keep all the plates spinning, exhaustion, bitterness, and burn-out soon followed. I learned a very important lesson through this experience: there truly is only one missional community in the world. If Jesus is the light of the world, we are at best a one-watt flickering light bulb. There is only one God in this cosmos, and you, I, and our church communities are not him.

It's easy to forget how adamant Jesus was in insisting on our need for rescue and resurrection. We don't need a guide or a role model; rather, we need a Savior. Jesus has graciously invited us to join him as he unfolds his finished work to those around us. Imagine a young child with a Fisher Price bubble-making lawn mower following along behind his father who's actually the one cutting the grass. This is the vision I wish I would have come to Chicago with. Our God is the One actually doing the work. No one can bear the yoke of being the Christ or emulating the Trinity.

TAKE YOUR FREEDOM SERIOUSLY

I know we keep pounding the same drum, but it bears repeating that we really are free (Gal. 5:1). And we should be grateful we are, not fearful. In our opinion, it's easy to focus on preserving the models made for yesterday rather than taking our freedom seriously in considering how we might be the Church today.

With the national disinterest in church gatherings growing, there is no better time than now to consider afresh how a liberated community of indiscriminate grace can be the Church on behalf of the world. To stoke our imagination, let's take Alcoholics Anonymous as an example.

LEARNING FROM AA

Alcoholics Anonymous has no titles, no budgets, no paid staff, no properties, no leadership ladder to climb, no currency for bartering in the public square, and no illusion of leaving behind a shining legacy. It meets in the basements of other people's buildings and uses their coffee pots to brew the bad coffee they got their own members to spring for with cash donations. AA is so widespread, in part, because they provide broken people with unconditional acceptance and friendship in a world that holds them at bay. Even though sobriety is their goal, their only guarantee is belonging.

Committed to being a shelter from the storm instead of an inner circle for the victorious, AA has flipped the script on what it means to qualify for love, grace, and community. As a home for people who have tried everything and lost, they offer a culture of tangible dependency, shocking transparency, and indiscriminate hospitality. These characteristics make AA stand in prophetic contrast to the many churches that offer belonging together with conditions to meet and checklists to keep.

LIFE IN THREE SPACES

At this point, you might be expecting us to introduce and unpack a church model. So, to prevent inducing an eye-roll, we want to share a couple introductory thoughts.

What we are about to propose has been used to help everyday people gather their friends around the reckless grace of God. It has also served leaders looking to start church families and spur disciple-making movements. In addition, it's been used by established churches, denominational leaders, and non-profits as a way to live and help others live as the body of Christ in the world.

We know it's robust enough to stand on its own, but inviting enough that anyone can learn from it and use it. The more important thing to us is that it leverages our God-given freedom to enjoy and extend the good news of Jesus alongside others. With that said, let us introduce you to *Life In Three Spaces*.

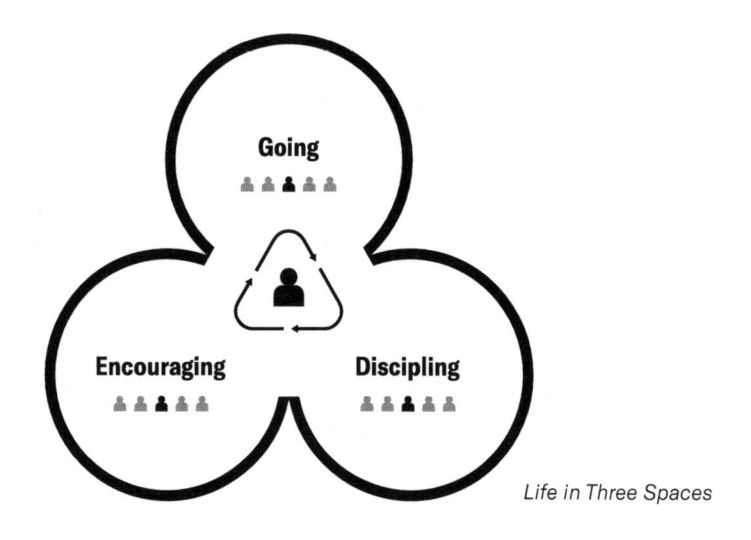

Life in Three Spaces

FIRST SPACES
Going To Others With Love & Good News

Jesus didn't choose to do ministry by planting and growing a gathering at the local synagogue. Yes, Jesus met Jewish people where they were by occasionally speaking in synagogues and in the Temple (John 18:20). Still, the fact remains that Jesus never established, maintained, or passed-on what would constitute a church today. In fact, his first visit to the synagogue as a guest preacher ended with his attempted murder (Lk. 4:28-29).

Instead, Jesus started with people. He was constantly on the go, meeting and interacting with people along the way. He was regularly in people's homes, having meals with them and reclining afterward for conversation. He did this with both sinners (Matt. 9:10) and disciples—who were also sinners (Matt. 26:20).

Looking at the way Jesus did things, it makes sense that we would find the freedom to frame our ministry in a similar way. If you recall from Reclaim 7, our ministry is to disciple others "as you are going" (Mt. 28:19-20). With this in view, the first space (as we like to call it) is about being present with those we know and love, sharing Good News as we go.

Think of this first space as existing in two major categories of social interaction: *Norms and Networks*. Norms are the following: the street you live on, your child's school, the local coffee shop you frequent, your workplace, your broader neighborhood, etc. These are the places you usually find yourself without adding a single thing to your schedule. Networks are different. These are the spaces where you intentionally connect with your tribe (those you share a common interest with). Networks include, but are certainly not limited to: the non-profit where you volunteer, the gym you belong to, the softball league you play in, your book club, the moms group you attend, the pub where everyone knows your name, the park where you skate, the pier you fish, etc.

In other words, First Spaces are the spaces you frequent and the people you're around on a weekly basis. As Tony and I have done ministry in spaces like these over the years, there are a few things we've learned:

Ministry Requires Slowing Down

We're not calling attention to minimalism or decluttering your life here but rather emphasizing how important it is to spend (even waste) time within friendships. In a culture that says "Go! Go! Go!" slowing down wages war on the values of productivity and efficiency.

Consider this definition of slowing down we crafted a while back: Slow Down (verb): to experience God's grace in such a way that one (1) abandons all visions of fixing themselves or anyone else. In this freedom, they (2) begin slowing down with people to love them over the long-haul with no ulterior motives and (3) enjoy those relational moments when they can share the same Good News that liberated them.

As you can see, slowing down has to do with sticking around long enough to see what God is up to in people's lives. The emphasis is on being fully present and attentive when you're with people. Slowing down also includes the margin to be a helping hand to others in their time of need. It's hard to really love others when you're racing by them.

Just remember, the most substantive and lasting things in our lives take time. Immediacy and authenticity rarely co-exist, if ever. Knowing that Jesus was socially labeled a "friend of sinners" provides us comfort as we give time to slowing down.

Become Well-Acquainted With Losing

In Luke 10, we find a passage often used by churches as a foundational text for their mission. But as we look closer, we see that this text isn't offering us a programmatic template. Instead, it's a much-needed lesson from Jesus about embracing our death as we are going. Jesus sends the disciples to nearby villages to announce good news of God's kingdom, telling them they are like "lambs in the midst of wolves." This isn't a reference to the dangers they will face but to their position in the pecking order of this world.

As anyone knows, a lamb among wolves is as good as dead. If the world were one big junior high school, Jesus is saying, "You're the losers," and thus dependent on Something far beyond yourselves. To help the disciples further embrace their loser status, Jesus even went so far as to tell them to leave behind everything that made them feel like independent winners—no money, possessions, or community (Lk. 10:4). Loving God and people is not something we crush but rather something that crushes us—and that's a good thing.

Share News, Not Advice

Our natural bent is to speak in the vernacular of law, not grace. "Do this" and "don't do that" is our native tongue. Or we just "should" all over people when they open up about some tension in their life. So remember, the gospel isn't a guide, a list of rules, or a to-do list. It's Good News about what God is truly like, what he's done on our behalf in Jesus, and who we are in him. In contrast, religion is advice for what we can do in hopes of finding God's favor.

SECOND SPACES
Discipling Those Who Are Open To The News Of Jesus

As Jesus went about sharing the news of the Kingdom with others, he also spent time with those who were OPEN to him. Whether it was a meal with people he was getting to know (Luke 15:1-2), dinner at Zacchaeus' house (Lk. 19:1-10), or a party at Matthew's house (Matt. 9:10), these became places where Jesus would connect further with people.

As the Church, we too are free to spend our time connecting with those open to hearing about what God is really like.

As people express a desire to learn more about the things you're sharing in everyday life, you will want to create a space where they can kick the tires of Christianity with no strings attached. Think house parties, dinner nights, lunch, coffee, beer, church services, guys night, ladies night, bible study, fishing trips, patio fires, etc. The key is that you offer an environment where everyone can come as they are and find a friend willing to walk with them as they learn.

As you think about Second Spaces for those you love, keep these things in mind:

Create Environments Conducive To Everyone

Take time to learn about those you are gathering so you can work with their schedules. We cannot overstate this. People naturally come together in anywhere from homes to church facilities, community centers, pubs, parks, art galleries, coffee shops, beaches or even break rooms. But they can only do so if the time fits with their availability. Church leaders are notorious for setting ministry times, dates, and locations irrespective of those they hope to reach and then wondering why people don't come.

Remember Why People Desire To Learn

No matter where you go in the world, you will find adults learning on a need-to-know-basis. When we move out of our childhood homes, we learn how to use a budget. When we start hosting dinners, we become interested in cooking shows. The list goes on. Remembering this will remind you to lead with friendship and listen to see where and how you can press in with others.

Some will feel comfortable navigating conversations in these spaces with nothing more than someone's question and a copy of the scriptures. In contrast, others may need to rely on other gospel resources to help facilitate discussion. To keep things simple, feel free to utilize the resources found through LARK or other platforms committed to the finished work of Jesus. Send out a link for others to listen to, watch, or read through a specific Scripture or teaching, then gather together to discuss insights and questions. Just make sure everyone knows what they're signing up for before entering or creating a Second Space. Things get awkward when an evening of wine tasting turns out to be a planned study and conversation.

Practice Hospitality

The word hospitality in Scripture literally means "stranger love." When you see yourself as a guest at the table Jesus has prepared, rather than an usher, you're free to view everyone else as fellow guests, not projects. You have no need to fix anyone or win them over. Instead, you get to just love them and help them feel at home as they hear about and experience the freedom found in Jesus.

THIRD SPACES
Encouraging Those Who Are Following Jesus

Many people heard Jesus unveil profound truths about God and life, but not everyone was eager to follow him. Along the journey, we see him gathering regularly with those who wanted to be a part of what God was doing in the world. We call these "Third Spaces"—gathering spaces for disciples to meet each other where we are along the way.

In general, the conversation of what constitutes a gathering of the Church invites passionate opinions. This was the case in Jesus' day and it remains true today. Over the years, people have sought to deconstruct, reconstruct, defend, and reimagine church. And we, no doubt, will now be adding our thoughts to the lump of dough. We aim to do so, however, without adding the Pharisees' leaven.

There's a scene in Mark's gospel (Mark 2:23-28) where Jesus and the disciples are traveling through a grain field on the Jewish designated day of worship—the Sabbath. As people often do when they pass by a field of food, the disciples pluck some heads of grain and eat. The Pharisees, who have begun to devote themselves to policing Jesus and the disciples' every move, begin to point fingers at the disciples for working on the Sabbath. "Look, why are they doing what is not lawful on the Sabbath?" (v. 24). In reality, Jesus' crew ate some grain that was on the fringe of a field—which wasn't wrong. It did, however, violate one of the 39 laws that the religious leaders had created around the fifth commandment. God originally ordained the Sabbath as a way to build trust and rest into the lives of his people. Why? Because he knows that our tendency is to not trust and instead, run ourselves into the ground with worry, anxiety, and over-work. He also knows we're frail and easily overwhelmed with life's various burdens. In short, God knows us and loves us, so he gave us the gift of rest.

After Jesus reminds the Pharisees that David and his followers basically did the exact same thing—they actually ate the ceremonial and hallowed "bread of the Presence" which was not lawful for anyone to eat but the priests—he hits these behavioral hall monitors with a line that's applicable for our current conversation surrounding the Church: "The Sabbath was made for man, not man for the Sabbath."

These religious leaders had turned something that was meant to serve God's people into something the people need to serve. To them, a worship experience was something to "get right" rather than a gift. Sound familiar? Some of us approach the conversation about worship on Sundays like the Pharisees approached worship on Saturdays.

We act like church is some puzzle to solve. We labor hard to fit all the pieces together, and when we finally think we've got it, we work hard to preserve it, protect it, and grow it. Before too long, we forget why we gather in the first place.

Why Gather?

Jesus' words in Mark 2 set us up to ask a simple yet important question: what is the purpose of our gatherings?

In Hebrews 10:24-25, we find a simple picture of what the Church did when they gathered.

"And let us consider how to stir up one another to love and good works, not neglecting to meet together, as is the habit of some, but encouraging one another, and all the more as you see the Day drawing near."

For centuries, church leaders have used this passage to guilt-trip people... we mean, remind them of the importance of attending church services. While we are all for church gatherings of different shapes, sizes, and styles, we do feel it is imperative to note what this passage is actually saying because of the opportunity it presents. Yes, the writer of Hebrews is pleading with these folks about the essential importance of believers gathering together, but it's the purpose of this gathering which makes it essential in our lives. So what is the purpose? Encouragement. Gathering for gathering's sake is not the point. Gathering to encourage one another is the point.

In this passage from Hebrews, the writer paints a picture of the early Church gathering as a "space" that honestly looked a lot like what Jesus did with his disciples. It was a safe space where everyday people could participate in the acts of love and discipleship we discussed in Reclaim 6. "Let us stir one another up to love and good works" and "encouraging one another" point to mutual participation. This participation wasn't commanded for the Church when it gathered, but it was described (Romans 15:14; 1 Corinthians 14:26). It was as if they were saying, "Life and loving others is hard, and you will need encouragement along the way. So gather with others when and where you can."

With these things in mind, here are some things you may find helpful as you look to offer a Third Space for those who are following Jesus:

Embrace The Simplicity Of Shared Meals

Are you really free to just imagine being the Church around friendships and shared meals? Yes. Yes, you are. Friends, this is not missiological rocket science. Not only did "the Son of Man come eating and drinking," but we also see the early Christians gathering around meals (Acts 2:46; 20:7a). A basic human need is three square meals a day, and a basic human phenomenon is the ability of a meal to bring people together. In 1 Corinthians 11:26, Paul, referring to what Jesus told the disciples, says, "For as often as you [gather together to] eat this bread and drink this cup, you proclaim the Lord's death until He comes." Jesus turned not just an annual meal (the Passover) but every meal into a sacred occasion for people to toast to and remember this amazing grace.

The Liturgy Of The Free

We understand how much of a shift this is for some of you. Moving away from a western-normative style church gathering can initially feel like you're walking away from Jesus himself. We know that feeling.

Hopefully, as we've shown from Scripture, you can find freedom and comfort knowing there is no universal prescribed form of public worship (liturgy). We really are free to create a culture of encouragement around the Good News of Jesus within friendships and shared meals—just as Jesus did. So, for those who desire to do just that, here are a few simple practices you may find helpful. Feel free to choose two, three, or all five of them.

> *Create*
> The first thing you will need to do is nail down a time and place. Showing up to encourage one another in Good News starts with a safe place for people to gather. Homes are the most simple, but you can gather people anywhere: parks, pubs, art galleries, cafes, community centers, you name it.
>
> *Eat*
> Like the secrets to good cooking, the kingdom of God is always hiding in plain sight. Perhaps this is why food mysteriously lifts eating beyond nourishment to friendship. So whether it's a buffet of chips and salsa you picked up from the grocery store or a rack of lamb with a cherry glaze, eat, drink, and be merry.
>
> *Listen*
> Because adults learn on a need-to-know basis, there's simply no way to encourage others "where they are" if you don't first know where they are and what they desire to learn. Having an ear to listen to those you're gathering will help you know where to start.
>
> *Contribute*
> Being encouraged and encouraging others is the hope of the Third Space. Here, we receive, and we also participate. Participation comes in many forms: hospitality, stories, Scripture, prayer, and even a song. Encouraging others to join is helpful—requiring them to do so is not. That's forced fruit. Simply give everyone who wants to participate a chance to do so.

Remember
There's a lot you can remember when you gather, but one thing is paramount: the One who gave His life for ours. Since Jesus gave his life for all, all are welcome to participate in the faith act of communion. Eugene Peterson said it well: "Not everyone can comprehend a doctrine, not everyone can obey a precept, but everyone can eat a piece of bread, drink a cup of wine, and understand a simple statement—my body, my blood."

Grace Strenghtens The Heart

One last thing. Since we're on a bit of a Hebrews kick in this chapter, we want to draw your attention to a potent little phrase in Hebrews 13:9. It's found amidst the author's closing words. It reads this way: "Do not be led away by diverse and strange teachings, for it is good for the heart to be strengthened by grace..."

It's a common misunderstanding to think that those in First and Second Spaces need the Good News of Jesus, but those who already "get it" (in Third Spaces) need more profound and "meaty" content for our ongoing encouragement. What a lie. The same grace that saves is the same grace that keeps our hearts encouraged and anchored to Jesus throughout life. Don't be led away from teachings that stray from Jesus and his finished work. Hearing about God's indiscriminate love and unconditional forgiveness in Jesus is the news we needed when we first began. It is also that same news we'll cherish most on our deathbeds. As broken people, we never really graduate from grace.

IN SUMMARY

Life In Three Spaces is intended to be a way to help people see how simple it is to be the Church right where they are. It's as simple as: (1) building friendships, (2) bringing those who are open to Jesus into an intentional conversation about Him, and (3) gathering those who want to follow Jesus to encourage one another—in the grace of God—along the way. Only one question remains: will you do so with the transparency and hospitality that flows from dependency?

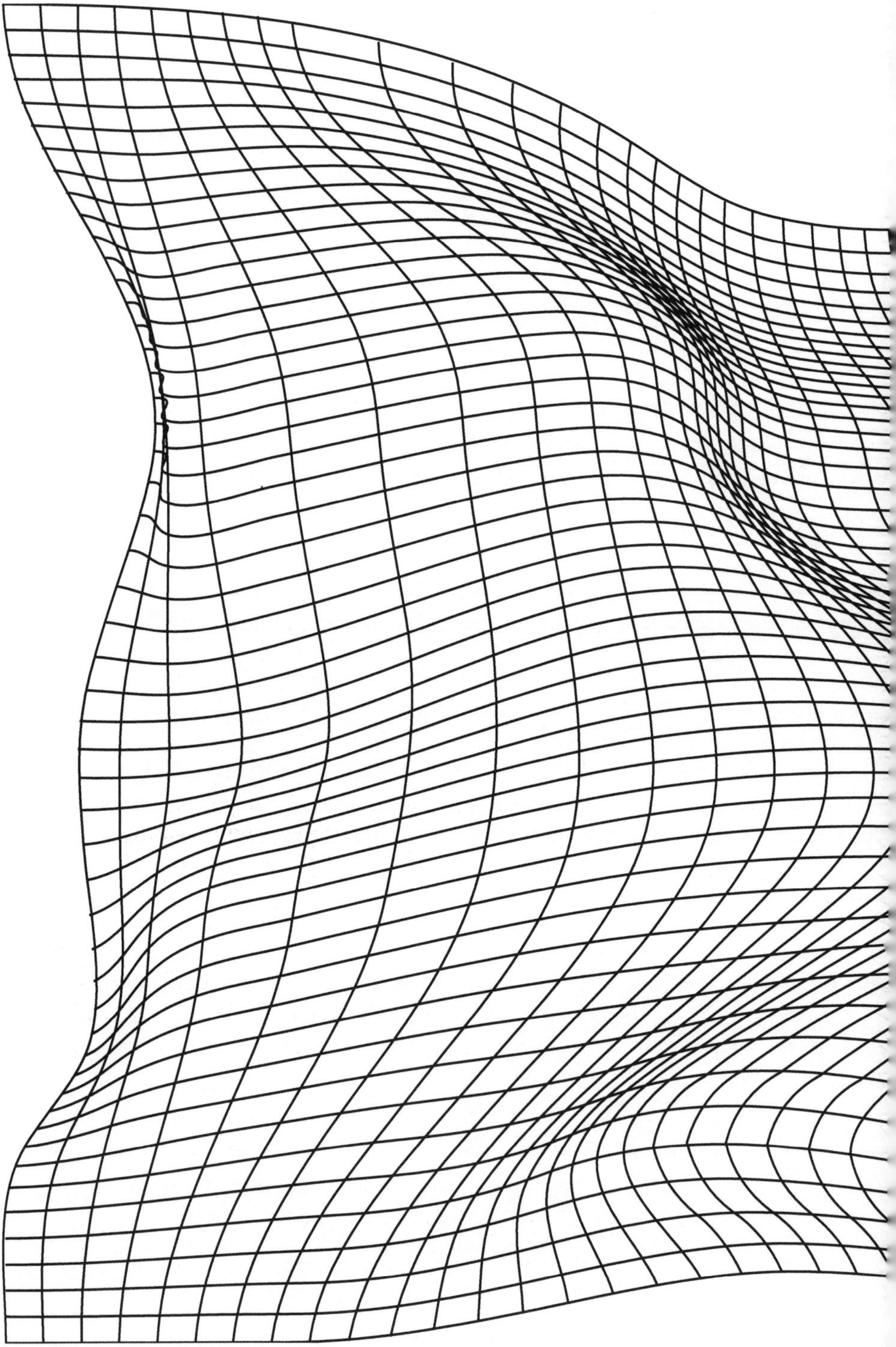

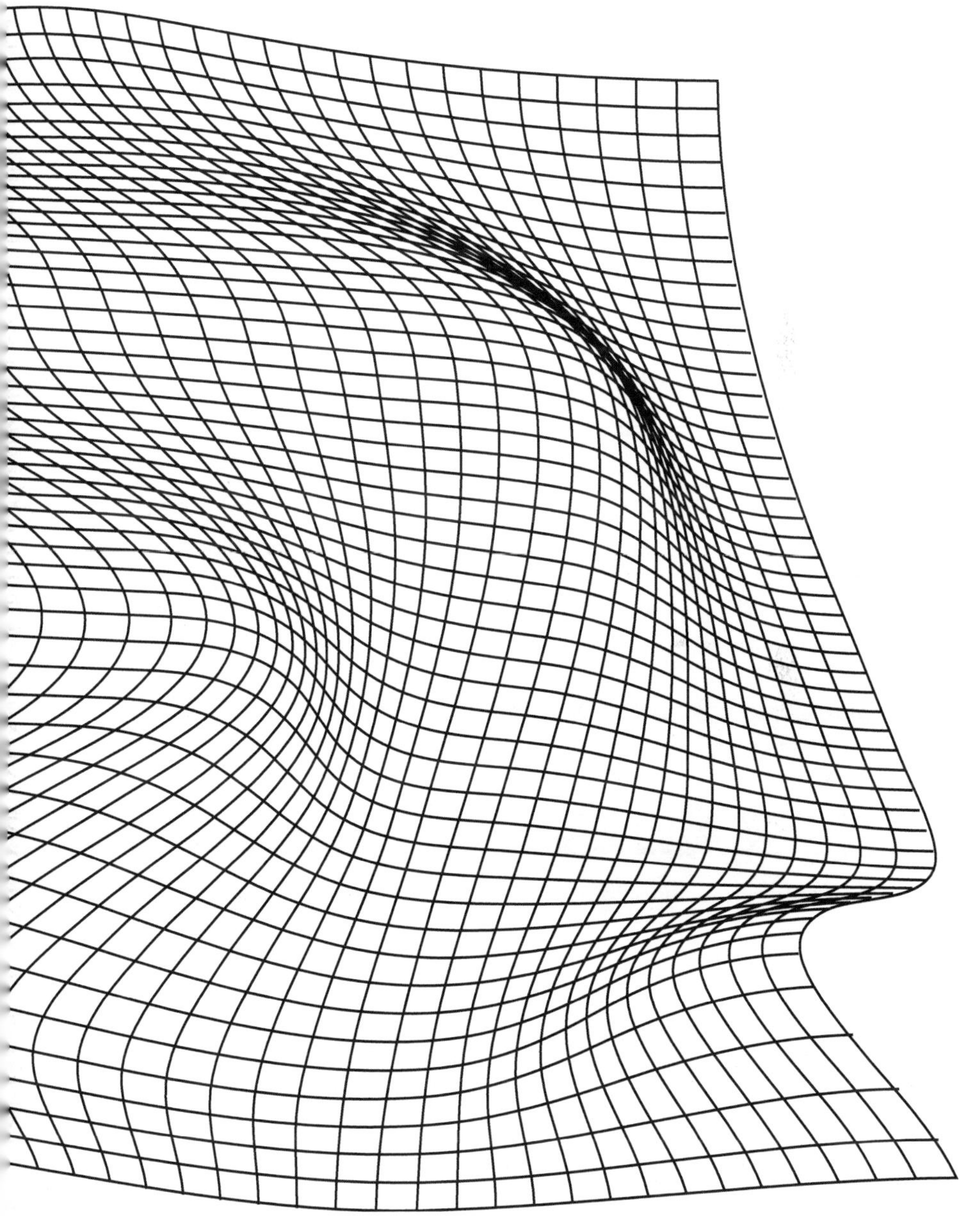

9

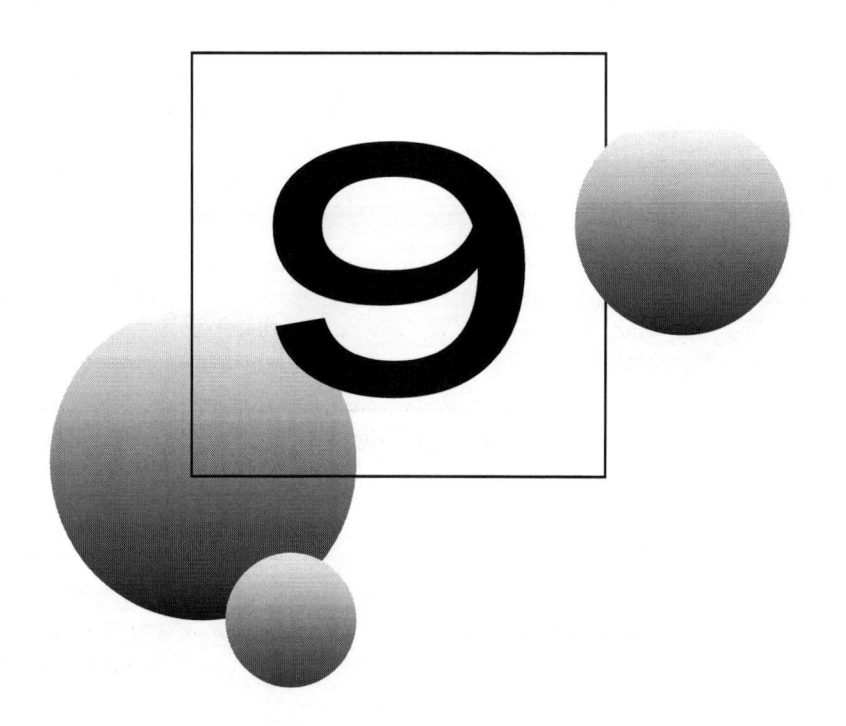

RECLAIM 9

PLAY

Whether you are a conference-goer or someone who grew up with a cultural understanding of church, chances are you think leadership is only for people with degrees and ministry jobs. So please hear us when we say that leadership is best defined by the word influence. To disciple others in Good News, whether you're helping a neighbor grasp the centrality of the cross or reminding a fellow believer of the same thing, is to lead them. And that's a work in which God has invited everyone to play a role (Mt 28; 2 Cor. 5:18-20).

The question is: how do we go about leadership and influence in a day and age when there are so many rules about what "role" we can play?

To answer this question, we want to end Reclaim with a look at Ephesians. Why? Because the city of Ephesus seemed to operate as a base for gospel movement due to its prominence as a hub for transportation and commerce.

Unlike other Pauline letters, Ephesians doesn't address specific leaders or deal with specific issues occurring inside this specific church. Due to its inclusive nature, many scholars believe Ephesians was a letter intended for the various expressions of the Church throughout Ephesus and beyond. This makes sense based on the connectedness of this influential city.

Theologian Markus Barth called Ephesians 4 "The Constitution of the Church" and considered verses 11-12 to be a mirror into how the Church functions for the spread of Good News. With this in mind, let's take an in-depth look at the text and observe the direct connection in Ephesians 4 between the language we encounter and the design of the Church.

THE CONSTITUTION
Looking At Ephesians 4:1-16

In Ephesians 4:1-6, we find a call not to create unity, but to "maintain the unity" the Church already has in the Spirit. To provide both a foundation and a framework for this call, Paul summarizes seven truths relating to our oneness: "There is one body and one Spirit — just as you were called to the one hope that belongs to your call — one Lord, one faith, one baptism, one God and Father of all, who is over all and through all and in all" (Eph 4:4-5). In Jesus, we are one.

In verses 7-11, Paul notes that Jesus "gave" (*edothe*) certain "gifts" (*charisms*, which means ministries given by grace) to "each one of us" (hekasto, which literally means "to each and every person"). In Paul's day, armies sent out to conquer new land would return with possessions that signified their victory. These possessions would then be handed out in their homeland as a form of celebration. Unlike those ancient armies, we didn't go and conquer sin and death. We couldn't. But we did, according to this verse, receive a calling/ministry as a "gift" that celebrates the victory of Jesus over sin and death. The gifts Paul references, translated "ministries," are tied to who we are, not what we do.

In verses 11-12, Paul unpacks these ministries/gifts, saying that Jesus "gave some to be apostles, prophets, evangelists, shepherds, and teachers" for a specific task: "to equip the saints for the work of the ministry." Let's consider the source, purpose, and result of these ministries/gifts before we address how Paul defines and describes each role. The distinctions are incredibly life giving.

APEST SOURCE

First, we need to consider Jesus, the source of it all. The ministries of Jesus when he walked the earth (i.e., apostle, prophet, evangelist, shepherd, and teacher—APEST for short) have been given to everyone. If we have been "crucified with Christ" and it is "no longer [we] who live," then our lives are in fact "hidden in Christ," as Colossians 3 makes so clear. This means that the ministries of Jesus we find in these verses are nothing less than Jesus making himself known through us, not vice versa. This is what Paul means when he says in verse 7, "But grace was given to each one of us according to the measure of Christ's gift." Nothing to strive for here, just something to walk in.

APEST PURPOSE

Let's also consider the purpose of these ministries that are given to all believers according to Ephesians. At the core of each ministry lies the work of "equipping" others. So, whatever ministry Jesus is expressing through you, Paul says, is not so you can be the star, but rather so you can "equip the saints" (i.e., other believers).

The "some" who are apostles, and "some" who are prophets, and "some" who are evangelists, and "some" who are shepherds, and "some" who are teachers—together—make up "all" of the Church Paul mentions in verse 7. When every believer plays their part, those around them are equipped by these ministries at work.

For example, living as an evangelist isn't just about sharing the gospel with people. It's primarily about helping every believer share the gospel with those around them. Being a teacher isn't just about helping others get rooted in their knowledge and understanding of what God has declared. Rather, it's about helping every believer teach those they're discipling to walk with Jesus.

APEST RESULT

In verses 12-16, Paul shifts his focus from what Christ gave to the Church to a description of what he will do in the Church as a result of us walking in the ministries/gifts he has given us. In verse 12, he states that the result of the body running in these ministries is, "... building up the body of Christ."

The Greek word Paul uses for "equip" is *kataptismo*, which is used to describe the act of setting a broken bone. Through APEST ministries at work in everyone, the Church grows in "unity" and "maturity" as "the whole body, joined and held together by every joint with which it is equipped, when each part is working properly, makes the body grow so that it builds itself up in love."

APEST ROLES

We now turn our focus to each individual role. It's our hope to define them in an introductory way and encourage their expression in your context.

APOSTLES

In Scripture, we know the Apostles as the founding leaders of the Church who personally saw and were trained by Jesus. Here, in Ephesians 4, we don't see the word "apostle" used in reference to the apostolic office but rather the apostolic wiring. In society, this aspect of God's image is generally seen in pioneers who love to start and drive new ventures. Thus, it is easy to see why the role of the apostle is characterized by the spread of Good News in new places. In short, an apostle's heart beats to see the gospel take root and grow in new contexts, and they will work towards that end. But note, if immature, they will bounce from one idea to the next, leaving people weary and unsure of where they are headed.

PROPHETS

In society, those with a prophetic wiring quickly see the gaps between what is and what should be. In the New Testament, they are not seen as "forth-tellers" of something God hasn't declared but rather bold proclaimers of what God has already made known in Jesus. They are always asking, "What has God declared?" As questioners of everything, prophets play a critical role in the Church by helping people speak grace and truth to one another. But note, immature prophets may act without love. They may interpret every action from the perspective of the law instead of grace (a right-handed approach). They may also find it difficult to trust the Spirit to produce fruit when and how he chooses.

EVANGELISTS

In society, those with an evangelistic wiring are often extroverts and persuasive salespeople. They are connectors who are always looking to create a positive encounter between people and the message of Jesus. Believing that God is calling people to himself and that every believer is an ambassador with a story to share, the evangelist must know that there is no one-size-fits-all approach. At times, they are exceptional recruiters who can get buy-in from their hearers, as well as social connectors who have the energy to build new relationships that lead to gospel proclamation. But note, an immature evangelist can dilute the gospel in order to not lose a connection or forget about people once they trust in Jesus.

SHEPHERDS

In society, shepherds are nurturers who often work in positions focused on the health of people or organizations. Think HR directors. There are many shepherd analogies in the New Testament, but at the core of them all lies the shepherd's desire to create stability. When looking at this role, keep two things in mind: (1) not knowing the people in one's sphere of influence probably disqualifies someone from being a shepherd, and (2) this ministry must always be seen through the lens of the mission to help others find freedom in Jesus' finished work. But note, immature shepherds will develop a gardener complex (see Reclaim 4), struggle to speak the hard truth when needed, and may find it challenging to spend time with those outside the faith.

TEACHERS

Teachers often have a great deal of influence, for good or bad, based on the platform God has given them. As creative thinkers who are concerned with theological truth, they work to bring wisdom and understanding into their context. One of the main differences between the ministry of the teacher and the ministry of the evangelist, prophet, or apostle is the sense of urgency—teachers never seem to be in a rush when it comes to things growing or spreading. But note, immature teachers often struggle to remember that knowing God—not gaining more knowledge—is the aim of teaching.

EXPRESSING HIMSELF THROUGH US, THE CHURCH

Now that we've looked at some introductory definitions of APEST, let's consider each role in light of the One who is making himself known through the ministries/gifts listed in Ephesians:

As an expression of *Jesus, the true Apostle*, who was sent from the Father to our broken world to rescue and prepare a table for us—apostles continue to live out the life of Jesus through an insatiable desire to see this Good News of Jesus spread to the ends of the earth—until there's a table on every street.

As an expression of *Jesus, the true Prophet*, who came on behalf of God to call us back to our Creator, Sustainer, and Reconciler—prophets continue to live out the life of Jesus by pointing out the gaps between what is and what should be in our beliefs and behaviors—so that the church would return to God's heart in this world and for this world.

As an expression of *Jesus, the true Evangelist*, who came to seek and save the least, the last, the lost, the little and the dead—evangelists continue to live out the life of Jesus by constantly connecting with those not living in the freedom and family of Jesus—in order to see them experience belonging and freedom.

As an expression of *Jesus, the true Shepherd*, who serves his people through constant care, protection, and guidance—shepherds continue to live out the life of Jesus by patiently walking with both people who believe and those who don't believe—caring for them and pointing them to truth and grace in their many seasons, whether joyful or difficult.

As an expression of *Jesus, the true Teacher*, who came to make known the unseen God through his life and simple truths—teachers continue to live out the life of Jesus through their ability to explain what God has revealed about himself to others—so that they too can know him and help others know him.

SOME COMMON QUESTIONS REGARDING APEST

In our experience, the APEST conversation is a new one for most. We wanted to take a quick moment to address some of the common questions we've heard from others when first considering Paul's words in Ephesians:

Are you sure these ministries listed in Ephesian 4 still exist?

Some believe that the functions of the apostle, prophet, and evangelist have been replaced by the canon of Scripture and thus are no longer active in the Church. Others disagree, claiming that this belief has led to an imbalance, as evidenced by the dominant culture of shepherds and teachers leading the Church. This culture has painted a very limited picture of Jesus to the world.

Here are a couple thoughts to consider:

1. In verse 7, we see the ministry of the apostle, prophet, and evangelist (along with the roles of shepherd and teacher) listed between the verses people cling to when calling for "unity" and "maturity" in the Church (Eph. 4:1-6, 12-16). It doesn't seem wise or true to Scripture to ignore three of the five roles God has designed for that end.

2. All five ministries listed in verse 7 (APEST) make up a self-contained grammatical unit of speech. Therefore, we cannot dismiss or even downplay one of the ministries listed without undermining the significance of the others as well.

We believe that the APEST ministries of Jesus in Ephesians 4 still exist today because Jesus is still expressing himself through his Church. The APEST ministries help each believer play their part, and as we function together, Jesus presents a full expression of himself to the world.

What about the other "gifts" we see in the Scriptures?

If you look at Romans 12, 1 Corinthians 12, and Ephesians 4, you will notice that the lists we often refer to as "spiritual gifts" are very different from each other.

Ephesians 4 uses the word kalesis, which means calling or ministry—as in something that is tied to our identity versus just something we do (e.g., the difference between a teacher and the gift of teaching.) Romans 12:4 differs as it contains the word praxis, which is associated with the things people do within a church family. Lastly, 1 Corinthians 12:7 differs as it is shaped by the word phanerosis, which connects the gifts listed with a gathering of the Church.

To summarize, we see in Ephesians 4 a list of ministry identities given to the Church by Jesus, not gifts of the Spirit specific to tasks within the Church.

GETTING STARTED

Many believe the limited movement of the Church in the West is With the perspective and practices found in Ephesians 4, it's easy to find yourself struggling with the paralysis of analysis. We know firsthand what that is like. So to close out this chapter on play, here are three things we have found that keep things clear and simple:

1. Liken the ministries of Jesus to a fire. Some people are best at starting fires from scratch (apostles); some know where to start fires (prophets); some bring others to the fire so they can join in on the party (evangelists); some keep fires healthy so they burn brightly (shepherds); and some protect fires from things that can put them out (teachers).

2. Picture the ministries of Jesus in two different camps for the sake of simplicity: Catalysts and Coaches. It seems that those with an apostolic, evangelistic, or prophetic wiring (although different in how they're expressed) thrive by functioning as catalysts for new ventures. They need the freedom to run. Shepherds and teachers seem to thrive as coaches within ministry endeavors. They love to create a community base because they know life is more like a marathon than a sprint.

3. Run in what you are naturally passionate about, and as you do, see what ministry Jesus seems to be expressing through your life. Think about what you love, what you cry about, what you would do if you were free of all the things you think you "should" and "must" do. Then, go do it.

Whoever you are, wherever you're at in your journey, you are free to play along in the work God is doing in others' lives. You will learn as you go. He's that good.

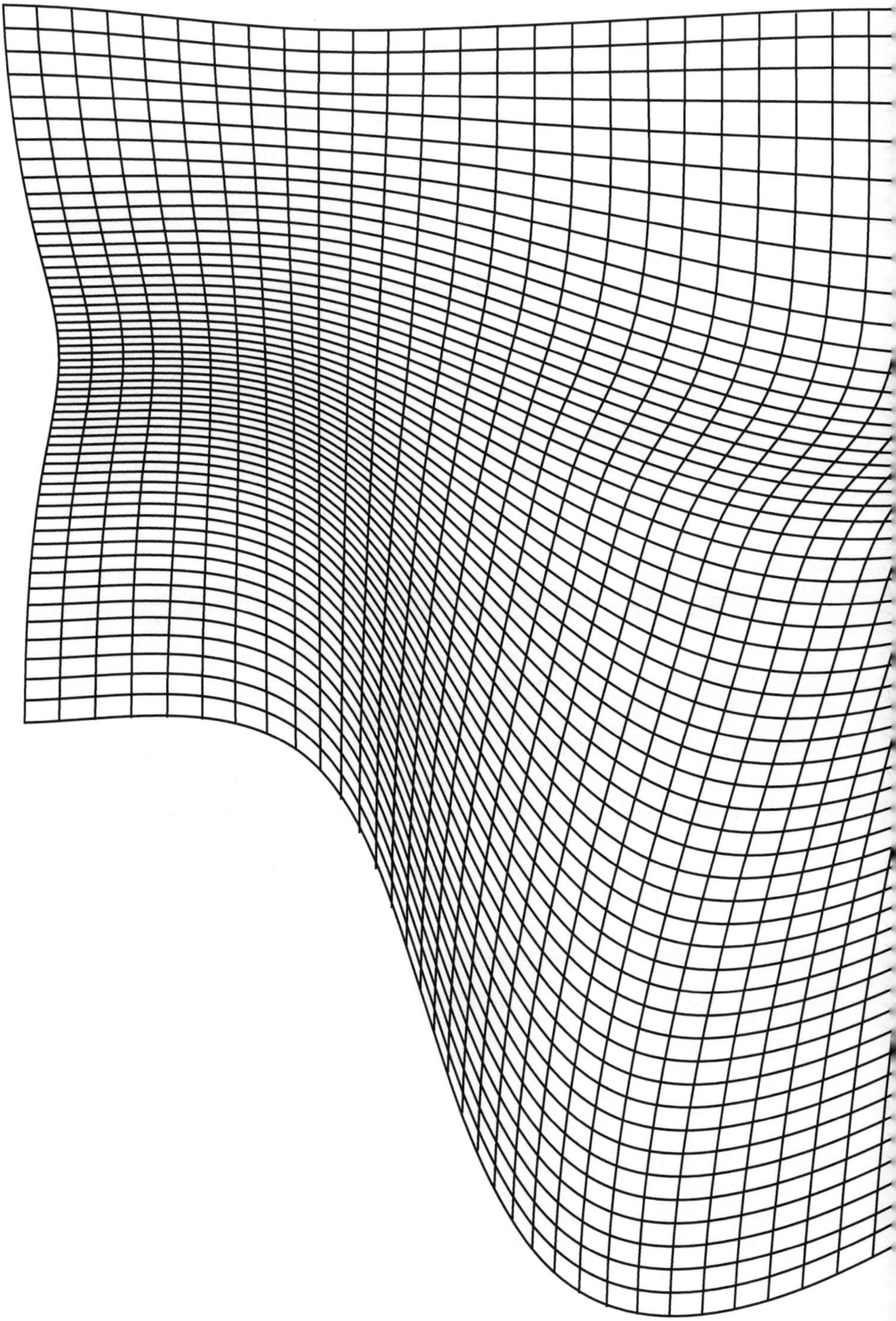

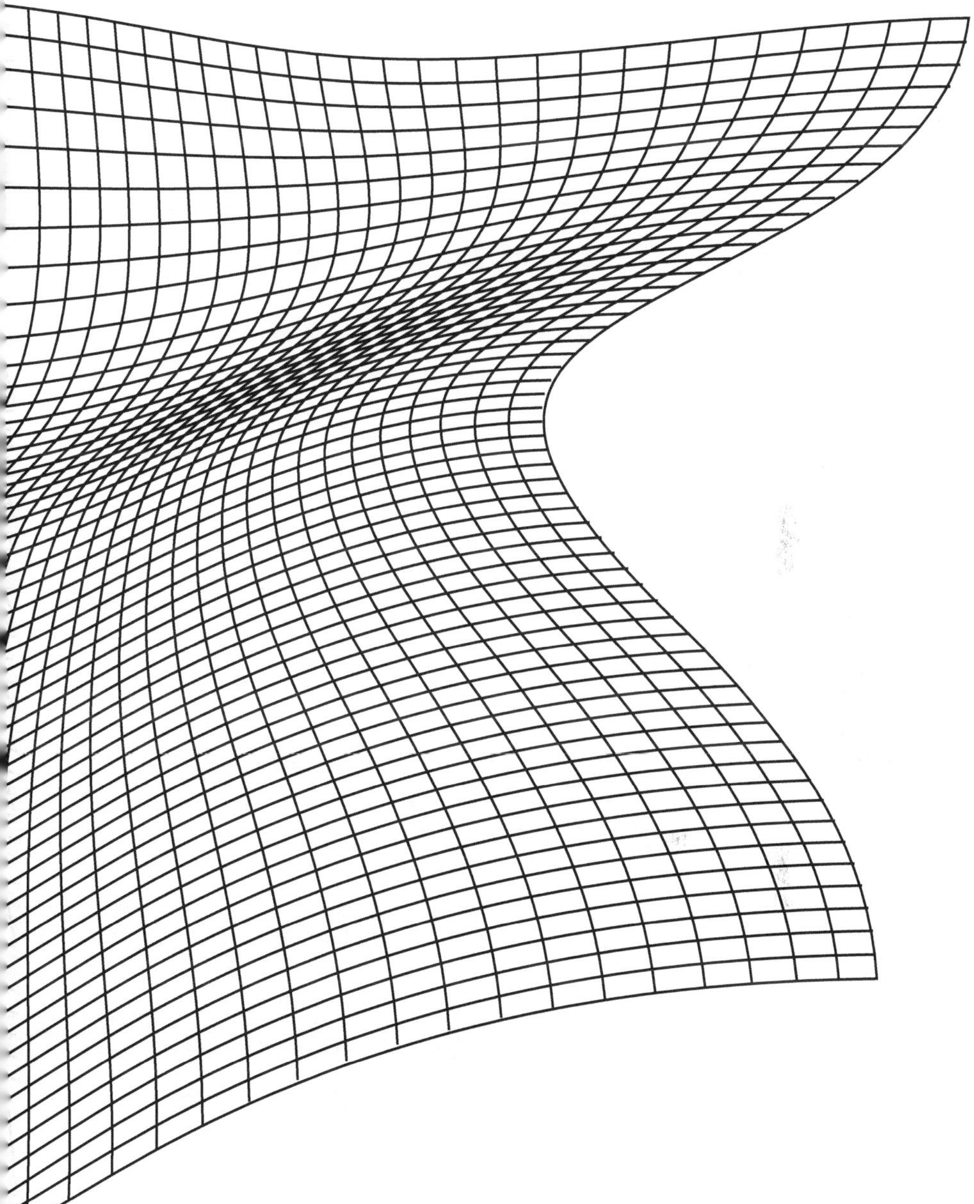

God, Who Through Christ Reconciled Us To Himself... Gave Us The Ministry Of Reconciliation.

2 Corinthians 5:18

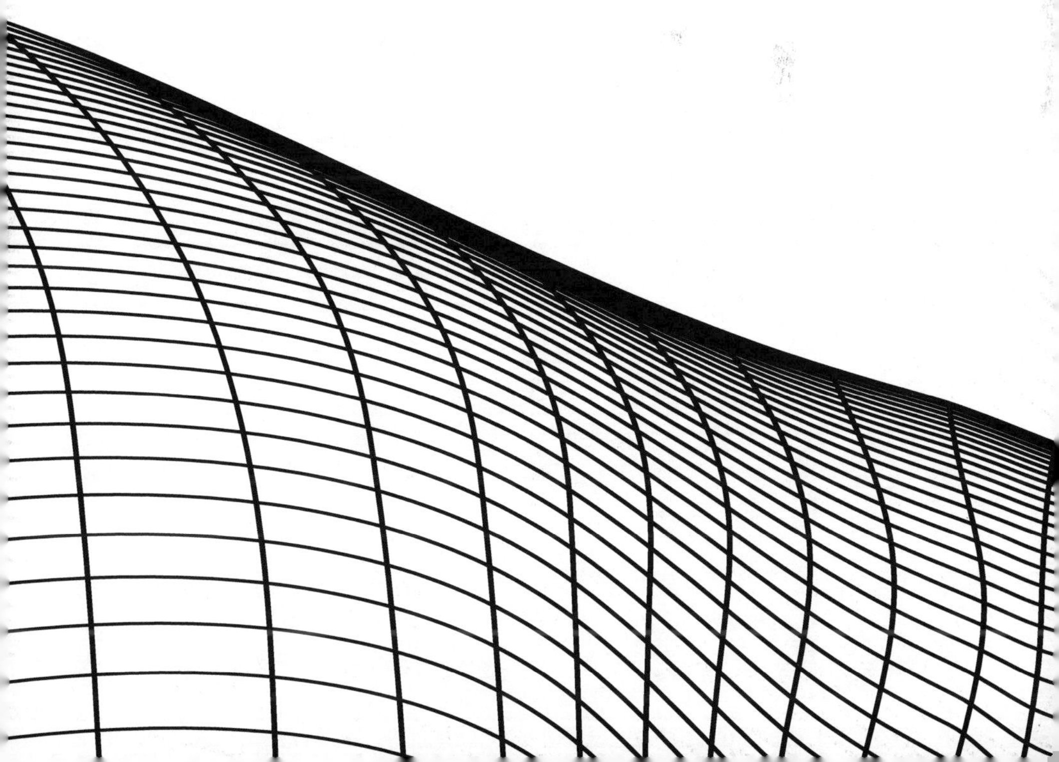

REFLECT
REFLECT
REFLECT
REFLECT
REFLECT
REFLECT
REFLECT
REFLECT
REFLECT
REFLECT
REFLECT
REFLECT

R.1

REFLECT

Reclaim
Chapter 1
Title: Jesus

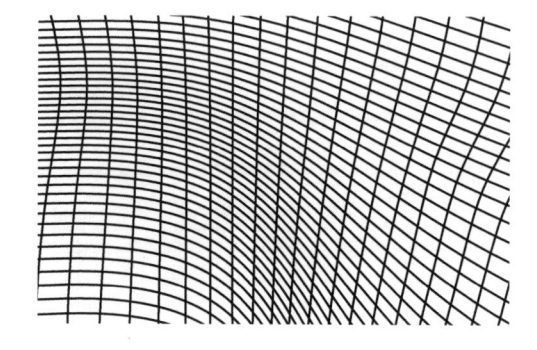

MAIN IDEA

Independence is a myth. Jesus is the creator and sustainer of all people regardless of their beliefs about Him. The gospel, therefore, is the actual good news that Jesus has reconciled "all things" in the cosmos and set a table before the world.

SUMMARY

Jesus is God the Son, the Word who became flesh and dwelled among us (Jn. 1:1, 14). He is the Truth, not a truth. The Scriptures are true because they testify to the Truth who goes by the name Jesus (Jn. 14:6). Since he is the Life himself, believing there is life independent from Jesus is a myth. Paul told the philosophers of his day, "for in him we live and move and find our being" (Acts 17:28). He is the creator, sustainer, and reconciler of everything and everyone, regardless of whether they trust him or not. (Col. 1:15-20) Jesus is King, the reconciler of everything, whose "kingdom is at hand" everywhere because he is everywhere (Mk. 1:15). No person, or thing, or place exists outside of him in this world he created. Nobody has ever built or brought the Kingdom where the King wasn't already fully present and reigning in the resurrected Christ. (Matt. 13:1-9)

SCRIPTURES

- The (King)dom is near and accessible — change your mind.
  [Mk. 1:14-15 + Lk. 11:20]

- Jesus is the Way and the Truth. He is also the Life.
  [Jn. 14:6]

- In Him we all live and breathe and have our being.
  [**Acts 17:24-29**]

- Jesus is the Creator, Sustainer, and Reconciler of all things.
  [**Col. 1:15-20**]

- The (King)dom is sown throughout the entire world.
  [**Matt. 13:1-9 + Matt. 13:44-49**]

QUESTIONS

- In light of Reclaim 1, how has your understanding of the "Kingdom" been challenged or affirmed?

- What, about your view of God's love, changes to know Jesus still sustains everyone's life, even those who persist in unbelief?

- Colossians 1 says that Jesus has "reconciled all things." How has this contributed to your understanding of the gospel?

- The King(dom) of God is sown throughout the whole world. Does this change your approach in reaching your neighbors?

R.2

REFLECT

Reclaim
Chapter 2
Title: Cross

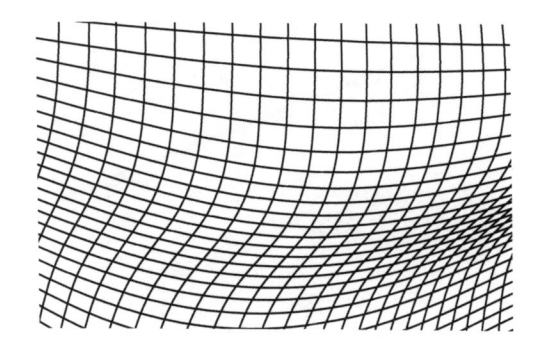

MAIN POINT

The mission of Jesus was to die (left-handed power). The only way to deal with sin—and the world it marred—was to bear it all alone in death, forgive it, and raise it up to new life.

SUMMARY

Jesus was perfectly capable of opening the proverbial "can" on all the world's evil. Instead, He seemed content to heal, love, and share good news over meals. Even those closest to Jesus wondered why He wouldn't wipe out Rome and take over in a display of what Martin Luther referred to as "right-handed power." God chose a path of left-handed power, which is intervention having an appearance of non-intervention, winning disguised as losing, and most struggled with this, even John the Baptist (Matt. 11:2-6). Jesus knew His mission was to die. He knew that wars, miracles, parables, and embarrassing Pharisees wouldn't fix a sin-sick world. Instead, He died to forgive us, an act so powerful you can't undo or reverse it. On the cross, Jesus announced His Father's dealings with the sin problem of this world as: "finished" (Jn. 19:30). Nothing has happened or will ever happen that has not been justly punished in the slain Savior of the world. The religion shop is now closed and the celestial bookkeeping department has been placed on permanent leave. In its place, a table was set before the world with an invitation to come and dine.

SCRIPTURES

- The Jewish expectation of the Messiah's coming was associated with judgment and right-handed power.
  [Is. 9:6-7 + Matt. 3:11-12]

- Jesus knew His mission — a perfect fit with His job description.
  [Matt. 1:21 + Matt. 16:21]

- Jesus came to serve, not to be served.
  [Mk. 10:45]

- On the cross, Jesus announced His Father's dealings with the sin problem of this world are "finished."
  [Jn. 19:28-30]

- Our sin was placed on Christ and, by faith, the very righteousness and perfection of Jesus are placed on us.
  [2 Cor. 5:21]

QUESTIONS

- In what ways can you relate to the Jewish expectations of Jesus and the thirst for "right-handed power"? Where do you see this kind of power at work in your relationships?

- The mission of Jesus, while on earth, was not to fix the Roman Empire or the world through military tactics, inspiration, or discipleship. Rather, He chose to bear the sin of the world alone in death and forgive it. How is this good news to you? How might it be good news to your neighbors?

- Regarding the misunderstanding that it's our job to "build" or "advance" the kingdom: What changes when you shift from seeing yourself as the general contractor of a major missional project in your city to approaching discipleship as a guest at the table Jesus prepared?

- How does the gospel challenge the hyper-focus of both the personal and social forms of Christianity?

R.3

REFLECT

Reclaim
Chapter 3
Title: Trust

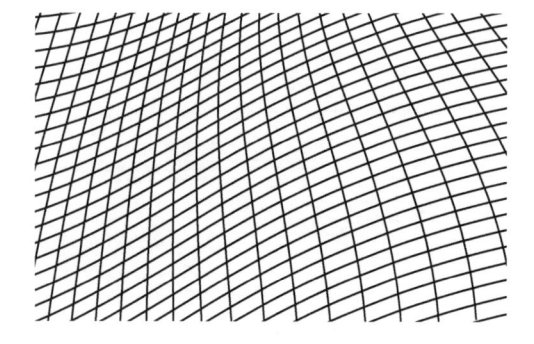

MAIN POINT

Our bent toward right-handed power in relationships must be contested and undone. Jesus—not only in His dying and rising, but also in His parables—is constantly showing us that salvation and sanctification are about believing, not behaving.

SUMMARY

In Reclaim 2, we pointed out that God (who prefers left-handed over right-handed power) decided against judging a hell-bent world. Instead, He died to forgive it. We bring this up again because only the constant reminder of this Good News will defend us against our bent towards thinking and believing there has to be something more than faith alone that makes someone a disciple of Jesus. Whether we like it or not, we are prone to behavior-adjusting as both a means of obtaining or maintaining our salvation, and in how we approach discipling our neighbors. Knowing this, Jesus constantly shares parables that undermine this performance-based propensity by rewarding the least performing (even ill-performing) characters.

The parable in focus for Reclaim 3 is the parable of the Pharisee and tax collector. In this parable, the impressive religious resume of the Pharisee is rejected while the tax collector's admittance of death and need for mercy is rewarded with justification. To drive home the fact that even the most gracious among us secretly love religious resumes, we give you a little test based on this parable in Luke 18:9-14. The main point of Reclaim 3 is to drive home the main point of Reclaim 2: salvation is about faith in the work of God on our behalf, not behaving better!

SCRIPTURES

- We need resurrection, not improvement.
  [**Eph. 2:1-7 + Rom. 7:24-25**]

- Jesus is our "once for all" solution for sin. In Him, we are already perfect.
  [**Heb. 7:26-27 + Heb. 10:11-14**]

- God saves on the basis of belief in Jesus, who came to save the world not condemn it.
  [**Jn. 3:16-18**]

- Salvation is by grace alone, through faith, in Christ alone.
  [**Eph. 2:8-9**]

- In the kingdom of God, religious resumes are not allowed.
  [**Lk. 18:9-14**]

QUESTIONS

- As humans, we resort to motive-correcting and behavior-adjusting as a means of obtaining and/or maintaining salvation. How did the Parable of the Pharisee and the tax collector challenge this bent toward performance and resume building in you?

- Regarding Luke 14:25-27, how did Reclaim 3 challenge your previous views regarding becoming or being a disciple? What was your previous understanding of phrases like "take up your cross"?

- After reading Reclaim 3, how would you describe the role of faith in becoming a disciple?

- Can you describe your previous understanding of grace and how it related to becoming and being a disciple? Did you experience any "aha" moments when considering the reality of grace in Reclaim 3?

R.4

REFLECT

Reclaim
Chapter 4
Title: Rest

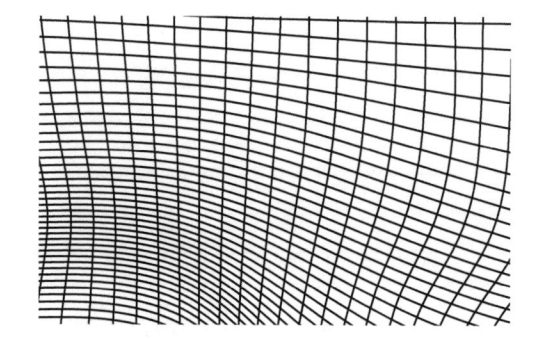

MAIN IDEA

For too long, a false narrative of improvement has plagued the Christian life, resulting in exhaustion among those within the Church and an increasing disassociation among those outside. The reality of the good news is that Jesus freely offers rest with the invitation to die to the project of self.

SUMMARY

Reclaim 4 is all about helping us connect the finished work of Jesus to our everyday life with Jesus in this world. This conversation of "sanctification" and spiritual progress has, unfortunately, been hijacked by what we call a "theology of improvement." Instead of seeing the Christian Life as a pursuit of progress (with a close eye on performance we can track), we shift our efforts and work as believers to trusting and believing in a Person who is "unseen" (2 Cor. 4:18). In short, Jesus is a Savior not a guide. Our work is under the banner of "It is finished"—knowing the life He's invited us into is neither religion nor irreligion. It's one of faith (Gal. 2:20; 5:6; 6:15). The parable of the two lost sons from Luke 15 illustrates this well. The parable contrasts the indiscriminate, insatiable, reckless love of the father with the sin of rebellion (younger son) and self-righteousness (older son). Instead of striving to be less like the younger and more like the older, we're invited into a life of rest, faith, and abiding. We're to die to the project of self and lean wholly on the Vinedresser and the Vine—the Ones responsible and faithful to bear fruit on our branches (Jn. 15:1-5).

SCRIPTURES

- There is no condemnation for those in Christ because there's no "you" to condemn.
  [Gal. 2:20 + Rom. 8:1]

- Like a tiny bookmark lost inside a gigantic novel, we are hidden in Christ.
  [Col. 3:1-4]

- We have already been sanctified. We are now seated with Him whose work is finished.
  [Heb. 10:10-14 + Eph. 2:6]

- You're a branch, not the Vinedresser. Branches don't produce fruit, they bear it.
  [Jn. 15:1-5]

- Rest is being offered to us by the One whose grace is sufficient.
  [2 Cor. 12:8-9 + Matt. 11:28-30]

QUESTIONS

- Do you think people in general associate rest with Christianity? Why or why not? What did you learn about rest in Reclaim 4?

- In Colossians 3:1-4 describes us as "hidden" in Christ, how does this truth connect to Galatians 2:20 and Romans 8:1?

- How was your view of bearing fruit challenged or affirmed in our discussion on John 15?

- In what ways have you found grace to be frustrating and/or freeing?

R.5

REFLECT

Reclaim
Chapter 5
Title: Walk

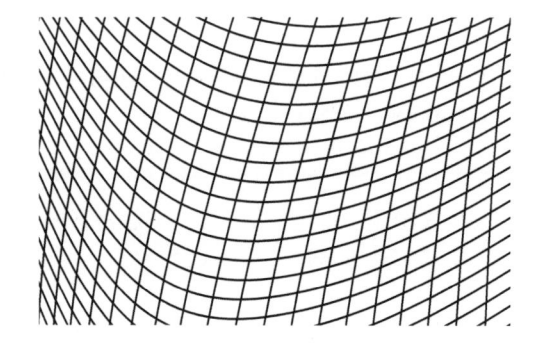

MAIN IDEA

Through God's gracious law the world can see what harmony looks like with Him and others. The good news is, in Jesus, this harmony is ours to enjoy. Fearful angst and fervent action is no longer the story of our journey; we have peace and patience as we simply walk in the fruit Jesus bears on our behalf.

SUMMARY

Contrary to popular belief, God has not given us a life of riddles to conquer, or ladders to climb. Instead, 1 Corinthians teaches us that God has given us a life of "faith, hope, and love." The world is steeped in religion. There is a tendency to see God as someone to please if things are to go well in life. Equating more knowledge and God's Spirit with our ability to measure how we're doing, map out ways to better things, and manage our progress as we go, is a failure to see how the law only offers us a picture of harmony, never harmony itself. This is why, by God's grace, the law also provides us with death, crushing our obsession with progress and pointing us instead to the perfect One in whom we dwell. It's in Him, by Him, and through Him that we can walk in the fruit we long for on this side of the veil. Reclaim 5 is about grabbing onto the truth that we have no need to pretend because we have no need to perform. We are free to rest as we learn to live by faith in the finished work of Jesus on our behalf. This is the Christian life.

SCRIPTURES

- The curious case of a free people who ran back to the law to seek a perfection that was already theirs.
  [Gal. 5:1 + Gal. 3:1-6]

- The law, inscribed on every heart, was always intended to show us our brokenness and need for Jesus.
  [Rom. 2:14-16 + Rom. 3:19-20]

- A life of faith, hope, and love is a witness to His grace.
  [1 Cor. 13]

- The law's ministry of death explained and experienced by Paul himself.
  [2 Cor. 3:7 + Rom. 7:18-20]

- Walking as a disciple is not a matter of do's and don'ts, but waiting, watching, and walking in the Spirit.
  [Gal. 5:5-6 + Gal. 6:15]

QUESTIONS

- What insights came from looking at the Galatian case study? In what ways do you see yourself in their drift from grace into the efforts of perfecting yourself or others?

- In 1 Corinthians 13, the Christian life is presented as a life of faith, hope, and love in contrast to the false maturity often found in lofty knowledge, spiritual disciplines, and showy works. In what ways does this challenge or affirm your ideas of Christian maturity and fruit in the Christian life?

- Which of these better describes your typical approach: (A) Map, Measure, Manage or (B) Wait, Watch, Walk?

- Describe how you typically deal with those nagging areas of your life where change is hard to see. How did Reclaim 5 change your thinking here?

R.6

REFLECT

Reclaim
Chapter 6
Title: Church

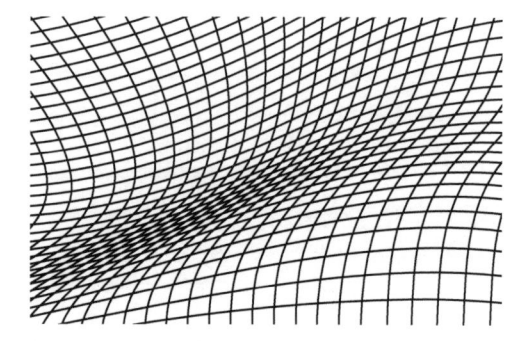

MAIN IDEA

The Church is who we are in Jesus (identity), not something we do or somewhere we go. When we believe this it sets us free from the demands of independent church structures and allows us to place our focus on learning how to live and love as the people of God in this world.

SUMMARY

Today, the word "church" has almost become synonymous with rented auditoriums, organized programs, well crafted sermons, and the popular leaders who champion them. However, the word "church" actually means "called out ones." Think: people, not place. We (the Church) are those who have been called out of unbelief, in grace, into the reality of God's radical acceptance of us in Christ. By faith in Him, our Father has made us ONE universal family, the "Body of Christ" in the world (1 Cor. 1:9; 1 Jn. 1:3). This is our identity. While most groups and organizations form based on commonality in gender, race, social status, or cause, the family Jesus forms transcends these commonalities, making brothers and sisters out of natural enemies. Capon said it well, we are "a random sampling of the broken, sinful, half-cocked world that God in Christ loves." To position ourselves as anything else "would be false advertisement." For this reason, we are free from the need to pretend or perform. We are free to be real as we learn to live and love in the One who has healed us. We are free to provide others a place to belong on their way to believing in the God who's also made them part of His family.

SCRIPTURES

- Formerly strangers, the Church is now a reconciled family. **[Eph. 2:11-22]**

- The Church is a mobile temple of everyday priests scattered throughout the world, who love well and carry the Good News of Jesus' finished work to all people in all places.
  [1 Pet. 2:4-5 + Eph. 2:21]

- The Church transcends commonalities found in gender, race, social status, or cause and makes brothers and sisters out of natural enemies.
  [Gal. 3:26-28]

- The function of our life together as the Church is lived out through the "one another" statements.
  [See "one another" scriptures]

QUESTIONS

- The NT describes the Church as a "holy temple" made of "living stones." What did you learn about the temple from Reclaim 6? How have you personally seen the temple's impact in your experience?

- In your mind, what changes when you shift from thinking of "church" as a series of behaviors to the collective identity we share in Jesus?

- In what ways have you seen churches widen the gap between itself and the world? In what ways have you seen churches narrow it?

- What truths, in Reclaim 6, have been helpful to you as you imagine extending the freedom of Jesus to your neighbors?

R.7

REFLECT

Reclaim
Chapter 7
Title: Disciple

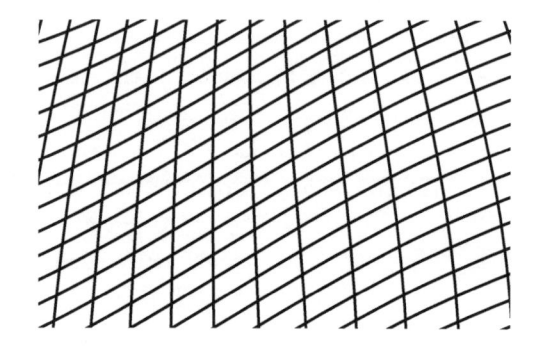

MAIN IDEA

Jesus has made every believer a "witness" and has given them the "ministry of reconciliation." The core of these acts is the call to love and disciple others as we live and move in Him.

SUMMARY

When studying Matthew 28:19-20 in its original text, the rendering is this: "Therefore, as you are going, disciple people of all nations, baptizing them..." With this first century understanding in mind, the pressure of a command is lifted and replaced with the natural organic flow of moving through life, watching for the Holy Spirit led opportunity to DISCIPLE! This translation removes the sense of compartmentalization of work, family, and ministry—bringing love and mission into everyday life through the ancient elements of discipleship: presence, listening, sharing, inviting, and teaching. So in a day where (1) most people are uninterested in attending a church gathering of any kind, especially ones not conducive to the tribes in which they identify and (2) will only give a listening ear to someone they know and trust. We have to put discipleship and the Church back into the hands of everyday people.

SCRIPTURES

- God is inviting the reconciled to share the good news of reconciliation. Extend to others what you enjoy.
  [2 Cor. 5:17-20]

- "Therefore, as you are going, disciple people of all nations..."
  [Matt. 28:16-20]

- "You are my witnesses..." points to identity first.
  [**Acts 1:8**]

- God became flesh and dwelt among us. This is good news and a model for presence.
  [**Jn. 1:14**]

- The indiscriminate kingdom—described as a net—is a good model for how we fish.
  [**Matt. 13:47-50**]

QUESTIONS

- What was your previous understanding of the Great Commission?

- How does the translation "As you are going..." change the way you view mission in the everyday?

- Which of the 5 functions of discipleship stood out most to you? How does seeing discipleship through this lens encourage you? How does it scare you?

- In light of the indiscriminate inclusion of the kingdom/dragnet parable, how does this change your posture toward your neighbors?

R.8

REFLECT

Reclaim
Chapter 8
Title: Spaces

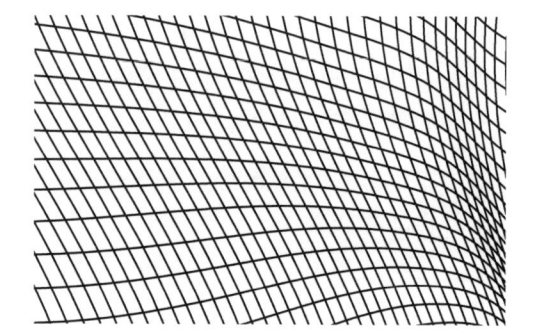

MAIN IDEA

Looking into the ministry of Jesus and the early Church that joined in the spread of Good News, we find an ancient approach to ministry marked by the message of freedom and the simple art of friendship.

SUMMARY

When 80% of society has no interest in a church service of any kind, we need something more than a "better" version of church if our heart is to meet others where they are. Seeing this, Reclaim 8 offers readers a way of being the Church known as Life in Three Spaces. It's as simple as: (1) building friendships, (2) bringing those who are open to Jesus into an intentional conversation about him, and (3) gathering those who want to follow Jesus to encourage one another—in God's grace—along the way. In this ancient, minimalist framework, the form of ministry follows the function of ministry, not vice versa; and your context gets to serve as the filter for when, where, and how things take shape. The only question is whether or not you will walk in this approach with the transparency and hospitality that comes from a place of dependency.

SCRIPTURES

- First Spaces: Going to others with love and Good News.
  [Matt. 28:18-20]

- Second Spaces: Discipling those who are open to Jesus (i.e. Zacchaeus).
  [Lk. 19:1-10]

- Go in dependence, not trusting in your own resources.
  [**Lk. 10:1-3**]

- Third Spaces: Encouraging those who are following Jesus.
  [**Heb. 10:24-25**]

- Third Spaces: A time for meals (communion) [**1 Cor. 11:20-26**] and a time for mutual participation [**1 Cor. 14:26 + Heb. 10:24-25**].

QUESTIONS

- In what ways did Reclaim 8 bring clarity or relief to you in regards to the gathered/scattered nature of the church?

- As you consider your norms and networks, who do you love and long to reach right now?

- How does the principle of "meet people where they are" change the way you approach these relationships?

- When you look at the myriad of ways one could participate in Third Spaces, what are some things you contribute to a gathering and why?

R.9

REFLECT

Reclaim
Chapter 9
Title: Play

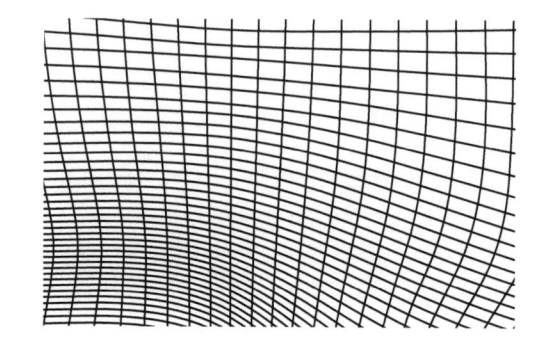

MAIN IDEA

There is no second string or b-team in the Kingdom. Instead, Jesus chose to carry out His various ministries through each and every believer. As we minister in and through the gifts He has given us, we equip and are equipped by one other.

SUMMARY

Sandwiched between the call for "unity" and "maturity" in Ephesians 4 we find the ministries Jesus gave to "all" people. The purpose for these ministries Jesus is expressing through us, Paul says, is not so we can be the star, but rather so we can "equip the saints" and be equipped by the saints running alongside us. As the "some" who are "apostles" and "some" who are "prophets" and "some" who are "evangelists" and "some" who are "shepherds" and "some" who are "teachers"… who together … play their part, everyone is equipped and maturity is found.
To see these ministries in practical terms, think of them as they relate to a fire. Some people are best at starting fires from scratch (apostles); some at knowing what type of fire to start, as well as when and where (prophets); some at bringing others to the fire so they can join in on the party (evangelists); some at keeping fires healthy so they burn brightly (shepherds); and some at protecting fires from things that could put them out (teachers).

Reclaim 9 is all about helping folks get a sense for how Jesus has wired them to minister in this world. Be sure to take advantage of the APEST discovery tool when helping others gain clarity about their wiring.

SCRIPTURES

- A theological summary of our unity in the Body of Christ.
  [Eph. 4:1-6]

- APEST is an expression of Jesus' ministries in the Body of Christ
  [Eph. 4: 7-11]

- APEST results in the body of Christ.
  [Eph. 4:12-16]

- Gifts given for service.
  [Rom. 12:4]

- Gifts given for when the Church gathers.
  [1 Cor. 12:7]

QUESTIONS

- In what ways did Reclaim 9 contribute to your understanding of the ministries mentioned in Ephesians 4?

- How does an "everyone gets to play" understanding compare to your past church experiences? How has this conversation changed your view of the Body of Christ?

- Which of the five ministries mentioned in Ephesians 4:11 do you identify with?

- How do you envision contributing to the gathered/scattered efforts of your church family in light of your unique wiring?

Authors

Russ Johnson and Tony Sorci collectively had 23 years of experience pastoring, planting, and leading in various church expressions until meeting in 2014. Russ had recently formed Table Network, with Tony joining him shortly after. For the next six years, they partnered in helping the Church get back to the joy of the gospel and its freedom as a people in the world. They transitioned Table Network to Lark and the Lark Collective in 2021. You can find more of their teachings at **larksite.com**.

RUSS JOHNSON

Russ Johnson is the Director of Lark, the creator and co-author of Reclaim, and the co-host of the LARKCAST. For the past 21 years, Russ has empowered the multiplication of disciples, leaders, and church families among those who had no interest in the church. Today he lives in Fort Myers, Florida, along with his wife, Christa, and their four children.

TONY SORCI

Tony Sorci is the Director of Content for LARK (larksite.com). He co-authored Reclaim and co-hosts the LARKCAST. His primary passion is to help fellow sinners find rest God's grace and joy in passing this good news onto their friends. Additionally, he founded a boutique creative agency in Northwest Indiana, where he lives with his wife, Pamela, and their four children. Tony is a tattoo collector, clothing/coffee/music snob, cigar enthusiast, motorcycle rider, and can't decide if his beard should be short or long.

LARK is committed to "Introducing God's Reckless Grace to a Religious World" through podcasts, videos, books, events, and a Collective that connects and empowers proclaimers of Good News.

larksite.com

Made in the USA
Monee, IL
17 August 2023